COPYRIGHTED MATERIAL — DO NOT DUPLICATE, DISTRIBUTE, OR POST

Contemporary Ethical Issues in the

Criminal Justice System

COPYRIGHTED MATERIAL — DO NOT DUPLICATE, DISTRIBUTE, OR POST

COPYRIGHTED MATERIAL — DO NOT DUPLICATE. DISTRIBUTE. OR POST

COPYRIGHTED MATERIAL — DO NOT DUPLICATE, DISTRIBUTE, OR POST

Bassim Hamadeh, CEO and Publisher
John Remington, Acquisitions Editor
Gem Rabanera, Project Editor
Miguel Macias, Senior Graphic Designer
Trey Soto, Licensing Associate
Don Kesner, Interior Designer
Natalie Piccotti, Senior Marketing Manager
Kassie Graves, Vice President of Editorial
Jamie Giganti, Director of Academic Publishing

Copyright © 2019 by Cognella, Inc. All rights reserved. No part of this publication may be reprinted, reproduced, transmitted, or utilized in any form or by any electronic, mechanical, or other means, now known or hereafter invented, including photocopying, microfilming, and recording, or in any information retrieval system without the written permission of Cognella, Inc. For inquiries regarding permissions, translations, foreign rights, audio rights, and any other forms of reproduction, please contact the Cognella Licensing Department at rights@cognella.com.

Trademark Notice: Product or corporate names may be trademarks or registered trademarks, and are used only for identification and explanation without intent to infringe.

Cover image Copyright © 2016 iStockphoto LP/no_limit_pictures.

Printed in the United States of America.

ISBN: 978-1-5165-2952-0 (pbk) / 978-1-5165-2953-7 (br)

COPYRIGHTED MATERIAL — DO NOT DUPLICATE, DISTRIBUTE, OR POST

COPYRIGHTED MATERIAL — DO NOT DUPLICATE, DISTRIBUTE, OR POST

Contemporary Ethical Issues in the Criminal Justice System

First Edition

Written and edited by

Jason Williams, *Montclair State University*

Liza Chowdhury, *Borough of Manhattan Community College,*
City University of New York

Evelyn Garcia, *Fairleigh Dickinson University*

and Robert Vodde, *Fairleigh Dickinson University*

COPYRIGHTED MATERIAL — DO NOT DUPLICATE. DISTRIBUTE. OR POST

COPYRIGHTED MATERIAL — DO NOT DUPLICATE, DISTRIBUTE, OR POST

COPYRIGHTED MATERIAL — DO NOT DUPLICATE. DISTRIBUTE. OR POST

COPYRIGHTED MATERIAL — DO NOT DUPLICATE, DISTRIBUTE, OR POST

Table of Contents

COPYRIGHTED MATERIAL — DO NOT DUPLICATE. DISTRIBUTE. OR POST

COPYRIGHTED MATERIAL — DO NOT DUPLICATE, DISTRIBUTE, OR POST

COPYRIGHTED MATERIAL — DO NOT DUPLICATE, DISTRIBUTE, OR POST

COPYRIGHTED MATERIAL — DO NOT DUPLICATE, DISTRIBUTE, OR POST

Introduction

The following text is composed in such a way that it sits outside the boundaries of traditional criminal justice ethics texts. While many traditional texts are often preoccupied with theoretical frameworks and the sociohistorical foundations that make up ethics, this particular text decidedly aims at contemporary controversies involving ethics and the criminal justice system. The coeditors decided to take this nontraditional route because aside from understanding the theoretical underpinnings of ethics and theory, there is a dearth of texts that conceptualizes practical realities within ethical contexts. Moreover, this text breaks from traditional textbooks by underscoring some of the major controversies that now permeate the criminal justice system (at all levels). Current issues within the criminal justice system involve racial–ethnic disparities, policing and training, community-oriented justice, mass incarceration, gender and familial issues, the war on drugs, and mental health. The chapters in this text will highlight an assortment of matters while paying close attention to the chapter's subject content. For instance, issues regarding race, gender, and class (among some others) will be addressed multiple times throughout the book. These variables will be highlighted for practical purposes, and this is done to introduce students to practical realities that they will likely face while employed as justice agents.

This textbook is designed to deliver information briefly but comprehensively. Chapters are written in a way that encourages critical thinking and dialogue within the classroom. Each chapter begins with an overview that breaks down the chapter topic in a comprehensive manner. Next, chapter authors cover selected controversial issues as they relate to the chapter topic. These issues are discussed in a way that encourages readers to think critically

about the issues. Last, the chapters are completed with a conclusion and discussion questions that are designed to help with comprehension of issues discussed in the chapter as well as in-class dialogue. Each chapter will have references included at the very end.

The first chapter talks about the recruiting, hiring, and training processes within law enforcement. Current controversies throughout society have forced training to the forefront regarding policing. The second chapter talks about police discretion and use of force. Police discretion and force has come under intense scrutiny from social activist groups like Black Lives Matter. Chapter 3 will cover issues of community policing and police relations—also issues that have come under intense scrutiny in light of poor community and police communications, particularly in inner-city communities. Chapter 4 will speak to the significance of community courts. While community courts have been in existence for quite some time, there is a dearth of information regarding ethical concerns of their use within the justice system. Chapter 5 will delve into the many issues surrounding the prison industrial complex and its impact on society, as well as the many ethical questions surrounding the prison as a viable tool against crime. Also, Chapter 6 will encompass an overall overview of the prison, mass incarceration, and prison culture. Most traditional texts fail to highlight the role of prison culture. However, this chapter will delve into this issue concerning ethical concerns. Chapter 7 underlines the role of gender and family in contemporary justice issues. Chapter 8 speaks to the ethical concerns regarding how drug offenders are adjudicated. Lastly, Chapter 9 will focus on the issue of mental health—also increasingly a major problem that many activist groups have been highlighting within social discourses and policy debate.

COPYRIGHTED MATERIAL — DO NOT DUPLICATE, DISTRIBUTE, OR POST

COPYRIGHTED MATERIAL — DO NOT DUPLICATE, DISTRIBUTE, OR POST

COPYRIGHTED MATERIAL — DO NOT DUPLICATE. DISTRIBUTE. OR POST

COPYRIGHTED MATERIAL — DO NOT DUPLICATE, DISTRIBUTE, OR POST

THE CHALLENGE AND DICHOTOMY OF POLICE RECRUITMENT, SELECTION, AND TRAINING

1

ROBERT F. VODDE, PhD

Reading Objectives

- Recognize the history and role that police play in maintaining social order and control
- Recognize the importance of establishing high standards for the recruitment, selection, and training of police officers
- Recognize the importance of recruiting and selecting police officers who are highly qualified, while at the same time representing the communities they serve
- Consider the value that a college degree provides today's police officers and the communities they serve
- Understand the importance that basic police training plays in preparing and conditioning police officers to effectively and efficiently fulfill their duties and responsibilities
- Understand that an adult-based, andragogical style of police training represents a more user-friendly, holistic, integrative, and collaborative approach to training that better serves the needs and interests of today's society

---

OVERVIEW[1]

Within free and democratic societies, especially within that of the United States, little if any consideration is given among its citizens to the concept or meaning of social order and control. Barring isolated or systemic victimization experienced by some segments of society, the majority of citizens take their safety and security for granted. While many books and definitions abound that address the concept of social order, succinctly stated, it is "the condition of a society characterized by social integration, consensus, smooth functioning, and lack of interpersonal and institutional conflict" (Schmalleger, 2015, pp. 9–10). While achieving social order within society represents the ideal—one in which all citizens coexist and live together in peace and harmony—humans, recognizing their own frailty, have instituted innumerable mechanisms that serve to control its collective behavior for ensuring safety, security, and overall well-being. Stated otherwise, *social controls* serve as the systematic practices that social groups develop in order to encourage conformity to norms, rules, and laws to encourage conformity and discourage deviance. Consequently, in man's quest for maintaining social order, there

---

1 A portion of this piece originally appeared in Robert F. Vodde, *The Efficacy of an Andragogical Instructional Methodology in Basic Police Training and Education.* Copyright © 2009 by Robert F. Vodde.

COPYRIGHTED MATERIAL — DO NOT DUPLICATE, DISTRIBUTE, OR POST

COPYRIGHTED MATERIAL — DO NOT DUPLICATE, DISTRIBUTE, OR POST

are hundreds of laws that serve to regulate society's collective behavior—with the ultimate goal of providing for some semblance of order and control and, ideally, living in peace and harmony with one another. While most members of society have been raised and *conditioned* to understand *right* from *wrong*, to be mindful and respectful of one another, and ostensibly understand the importance for law and order, they also recognize that when one violates society's laws, there is a consequence. Such sanctions—intended to be proportionate to the seriousness of the offense—cover a range of consequences, to include a warning, reprimand, fine, forfeiture, probation, imprisonment, and in extreme cases, death.

While most of society's laws are of a civil nature, criminal laws serve to protect society at large; for committing a crime is considered to be so reprehensible in its nature that it is not only an offense against the individual victim but an affront to all of society. Hence, if someone is alleged to have violated the criminal law, they are prosecuted not by the victim but by the government representing society at large. Recognizing that criminal laws are legislated by elected officials who, in principle, represent society's needs and interests, the enforcement of society's laws is left to the executive branch of government, which in the case of criminal laws, is relegated to the nearly 18,000 separate police and law enforcement agencies throughout the United States.

While the enforcement of society's laws and the consequence of violating them are essential to maintaining social order and control, the means by which our laws are enforced and adjudicated is equally important, especially within a free and democratic society such as the United States; one where its *Founding Fathers* thoughtfully acknowledged and advocated for the inalienable rights of its citizens as articulated within the Declaration of Independence and extended in the spirit of its Constitution and the Bill of Rights. Indeed, there is a delicate balance between safeguarding the needs and interests of society at large while at the same time respecting every citizen's civil rights. Maintaining such a balance is underscored by Hobbes, Locke, and Rousseau's *social contract* (Friend, 2004; Morris, 2000; Riley, 1999), for even in a democracy

such as the United States, there are limitations to the freedom citizens enjoy in exchange for the safety and security that government provides.

Notwithstanding the recognition that historically, the responsibility for maintaining social order and control began with one's family, and by extension the immediate community, as society grew, expanded, and matured, this responsibility was eventually outsourced to what has evolved into our current-day policing system. While policing throughout the world has experienced incremental growth and tumultuous changes, so too has the policing within the United States. In this regard, it is noteworthy to point out that the historical growth and development of America's policing have closely paralleled the growth and maturation of the changing society in which it served, thus underscoring the many challenges and controversies policing has experienced throughout the course of America's history. As historians attest, the United States has experienced a myriad of exponential social, cultural, political, legal, economic, and technological changes that continue to challenge and influence all aspects of today's society, not the least of which include the changing role, responsibility, and expectations of its police.[2]

To understand today's police, it is important to recognize that they are a microcosm of society; that is, they are a product of, and an integral component of, the communities they serve. This was perhaps

---

2   The historical synopsis of America's policing eras reflects the writings and summarizations addressed within the book *The Efficacy of an Andragogical Instructional Methodology in Basic Police Training and Education* (Vodde, 2009). This synopsis does not take into account how slavery, segregation, discrimination, and racism affected the development of policing strategies and how these strategies affected police response to minority communities. The history of America's police encompasses many components, including that involving the slave police of the South. The significance of this synopsis is to merely provide an overview of the development of U.S. policing, thus underscoring the parallels between police and society, and the challenges both encountered. It is important to acknowledge that slavery, segregation, discrimination, and racism have adversely affected America's policing and by extension the criminal justice system, a subject that warrants an independent publication.

COPYRIGHTED MATERIAL — DO NOT DUPLICATE. DISTRIBUTE. OR POST

COPYRIGHTED MATERIAL — DO NOT DUPLICATE, DISTRIBUTE, OR POST

best stated by Sir Robert Peel, often considered the *father of modern policing*, when he declared

> the police are the public and the public are the police; the police being only members of the public who are paid to give full time attention to duties which are incumbent on every citizen in the interests of community welfare and existence. (as cited in Ascoli, 1979)

Stated otherwise, and as Swanson, Territo, and Taylor (2001) point out, "as a profoundly significant social institution, policing is subject to, and continuously shaped by, a multitude of forces at work in our larger society"; thus, the history of American policing "cannot be understood properly if it is examined alone" (p. 1)—rather, it can best be understood in the context of America's growth and development. Similarly, as Brandl and Barlow (2004) point out, "social institutions, such as the police, are human constructions that form and develop in relation to various political, economic, and social forces" (p. 1) in which they operate.

Indeed, America's police have experienced a long and tumultuous history, which has been characterized as having evolved through four eras—the Colonial Era, the Political Era, the Reform Era, and the Community Policing Era (Vodde, 2009). Certainly, today's police cannot be abstracted from their past. On the contrary, their current standing within society has been forged over a long period of time, which speaks to how and why they exist and operate today. A brief overview of these four eras is apropos to understanding not only today's police, but more importantly, how their history speaks to many of the problems and challenges they continue to face within today's society.

(1995), addressing America's early police, writes that "in the colonial period, order maintenance and crime-fighting were more individual and communal responsibilities than the purview of a bureaucratic agency" (p. 554). Over time, however, as English colonists increased in numbers and their communities grew and developed, the means for maintaining social order and control was influenced, to a great extent, by the "customs, laws, and law enforcement systems known in their native land" (Champion & Hooper, 2003, p. 74, as cited in Vodde, 2009). While the positions and operational practices of the Watch and Ward system, the constable, and the sheriff served the interests of America's early pioneers, they "eventually acquired distinctive American features" (Walker & Katz, 2005, pp. 27–28) as a consequence of the many changes the country was experiencing.

While policing during this time was greatly influenced and characterized by what was happening within America's major cities, policing within the Wild West was associated with the use of local sheriffs and deputies, posses, vigilante justice, and the glamorization of individuals such as Bat Masterson, Wyatt Earp, Pat Garrett, and Henry McCarty (Billy the Kid); America's early policing "system" reflected a pragmatic response to the needs and interests of its local constituency. By most accounts, policing represented a disorganized, uncoordinated, and decentralized enterprise, due in great part to the colonists' contempt for a centralized government. This brought the police to local control, and by default, under the influence of local politics. Clearly, in retrospect, there was a conspicuous absence of any uniform or standardized mission, vision, goals or objectives, and training. Conceptually and operationally, any form of police training was ostensibly nonexistent during the Colonial Era.

AMERICA'S COLONIAL ERA OF POLICING (1600–1840)

The Colonial Era of American policing represented a fragmented history that was greatly influenced by its British counterparts, where the use of the *Watch and Ward*, constables, sheriffs and other similar policing practices were adopted. Bailey

AMERICA'S POLITICAL ERA OF POLICING (1840–1930)

Underscoring the historical parallels between society and its police, Kelling and Moore (1998, as cited in Brandl & Barlow, 2004) explain that the *Political Era* of policing was so named because of the contentious relationship that existed between

COPYRIGHTED MATERIAL — DO NOT DUPLICATE, DISTRIBUTE, OR POST

COPYRIGHTED MATERIAL — DO NOT DUPLICATE, DISTRIBUTE, OR POST

the police and politicians. Political corruption permeated nearly every aspect of local government, of which the police were at the center. As with the Colonial Era, it is important to bear in mind that its characterization is principally based on the activities that were systemic to America's major cities. This was due in great part to the influences of the Industrial Revolution, which attracted a large and culturally diverse influx of people to America's cities, both from its own rural areas and from countries such as Ireland and Germany. This convergence of social, political, and economic forces led to overpopulation, social unrest, social disorder, and crime. These problems were further compounded by the tragic and tumultuous effects of the Civil War (1861–1865) and the following era of Reconstruction. Not only did the population of the United States triple in size from 30 million to over 92 million during this period, but so did the number of people living in its cities.

Notwithstanding many of the positive aspects of this period, such as the close bond that the police had established with the community, this era was "characterized by politics, corruption, urbanization, industrialization, migration of people, and growth in public and private" (Roberg, Novak, & Cordner, 2005, p. 46). Addressing the adverse influence of politics, Roberg explains that several trends converged in the mid-1800s that resulted in the creation of political machines that controlled cities, including the police department. The influence of politics was so overt during this period, that it not only influenced police arrests and services, but also "who was employed, who was promoted, who was the chief of police, and who was appointed to the police commission"; in effect, the police department was run "in a manner approved by elected officials" (Roberg et al., 2005, p. 46; Miller & Hess, 2005).

By the end of the century, as cities began to grow larger and become more difficult to manage, the politically corrupt police departments came under increasing criticism. Indeed, the ill effects of the *Roaring Twenties*, Prohibition, labor strikes, the crash of the stock market, and the residual effects of World War I all took their toll. The public's growing contempt for political corruption and other social ills such as "an increase in crime, population congestion, inadequate housing, health problems, [and] waste disposal" all gave rise to calls for reform (Champion & Hooper, 2003, p. 85). The reformers, or *progressives*, as they came to be known, "were made up of religious leaders and civic-minded upper and middle-class business and professional people [who] argued that government should be managed efficiently, public officials should be honest, and there should be one standard of conduct for everyone" (Roberg, Crank, & Kuykendall, 2000, p. 45). Finally, as part of his initiative to reform government, in 1929 President Herbert Hoover appointed the *National Commission on Law Observance and Enforcement* (1929–1931) to study the criminal justice system, which set the stage for a new era of policing (Roberg et al., 2005).

AMERICA'S REFORM ERA OF POLICING (1930–1970)

Given the overreaching influence and control that politicians exercised over the police during the *Political Era*, there was a grassroots movement for change and reform by citizens and government alike. Society's demand for reforms gave rise to renewed calls for law and order, which also emphasized the need for professionalizing the police in the fight against crime (Brandl & Barlow, 2004). Champion and Hooper (2003), addressing the transition of policing from the *Political Era* into the *Reform Era*, suggest that two major factors led to the periods' growth and reform: the progressive movement and new technologies. The progressive movement, as it applied to government, was based on three basic ideas: (1) honesty and efficiency in government, (2) more authority for public officials (and less for politicians), and (3) the use of experts to respond to specific problems (Roberg et al., 2000, p. 45). Collectively, this opened the door to adopting the professional model of policing[3] (Vodde, 2009; Walker & Katz, 2005).

---

3 The professionalization movement of the Reform Era emphasized the following: (a) define policing as a profession, (b) eliminate political influence from policing, (c) appoint qualified chief executives, (d) raise personnel standards, (e) introduce principles of scientific management, and (f) develop specialized units (Walker & Katz, 2005).

COPYRIGHTED MATERIAL — DO NOT DUPLICATE, DISTRIBUTE, OR POST

COPYRIGHTED MATERIAL — DO NOT DUPLICATE, DISTRIBUTE, OR POST

By the 1920s, attempts at reform on the local, state, and federal levels were beginning to have an impact, particularly given the influence of Hoover's National Commission on Law Observance and Enforcement. A significant part of the commission's report was the product of volume 11 of the *Wickersham Commission Report*, titled *Report on the Lawlessness in Law Enforcement*, and volume 14 of *Report on the Police*, a 14-volume report that addressed, among other things, pervasive political corruption, police brutality, poor education, and training (1931).

Bailey (1995) explains that "the impetus for police reform" (p. 562) came not only from society at large but from within the ranks of the police themselves. These leaders concluded, inter alia, that "the police function was spread too thin and that the organization was a catch-all agency that absorbed too many social service responsibilities" (p. 562), arguing that these responsibilities detracted from what they saw as the primary goal of the police, which was crime control. Relying on a professional model, "police leaders pushed for more centralization in the administration of the departments by lengthening the chief's tenure, developed a model that organized the departments along the functional rather than geographic lines" (p. 562), and aimed at lessening political influences, thus insulating the police from politics. Paradoxically, while these changes succeeded in distancing the police from adverse political influences, it resulted in a more bureaucratic, legalistic, and professional model of policing—which at the time was welcomed by society looking for the police to restore law and order. Consequently, the subscription to this model stifled their ability to recognize and respond to social changes during the 1960s and 1970s, which once again led to calls for reform.

AMERICA'S COMMUNITY POLICING ERA (1980–2000)

Not unlike the state of affairs that prompted reforms by England's Sir Robert Peel in 1829 and those by America's August Vollmer a century later (Carte & Carte, 1975), the social climate in America during the 1960s and 1970s once again called for much-needed change, due to growing violence and civil unrest (Gale, 1996). Events such as the civil rights movement, Vietnam War protests, the *hippie, peace, and free love movement,* experimentation with hallucinogenic and other illicit drugs, a rise in the crime rate, along with a host of other tumultuous social changes, prompted unparalleled reactions on the part of the police (Schmalleger, 2015). Their conditioned response to the social unrest of the time was based on the mind-set and orientation of the *Reform Era*, which placed primacy on the need to reestablish *law and order*. Society during the time of the *Reform Era* not only empowered the police with the requisite authority as *crime fighters* but looked to them as recognized and respected authority figures within the community. While an authoritarian and militaristic response by the police to the social unrest was perhaps what society needed and wanted as a consequence of the corruption, social disorder, and lawlessness associated with the *Political Era*, this same type of response was met with contempt, resistance, and the police being characterized as *pigs*, storm troopers, and the *Gestapo*. Images of police in riot gear employing batons, tear gas, water cannons, and canines to quell crowds evoked not only complaints of police brutality but an outcry that the police were unsympathetically out of touch with society.

Once again, this gave rise to a call for much-needed reforms on the part of the police to reconnect with society, which, among many things, underscored the importance for more training and was articulated in the 1967 *Task Force on Police* as part of the *President's Commission on Law Enforcement and the Administration of Justice*. Among the task force's many recommendations was a call for a minimum 4-year college degree and an academy curriculum that emphasized due process, sensitivity toward the public, and "an appreciation for enforcing the law and maintaining peace in a democratic society" (Bailey, 1995, p. 528). Further, it was viewed that by studying the psychological and sociological principles of human behavior, recruits could gain a better understanding of the community, thus reducing hostility and consequently reducing citizen complaints and litigation.

COPYRIGHTED MATERIAL — DO NOT DUPLICATE, DISTRIBUTE, OR POST

COPYRIGHTED MATERIAL — DO NOT DUPLICATE, DISTRIBUTE, OR POST

While the objective may have been more pragmatically oriented—that is, with an eye on improving the measurable efficiency and effectiveness of the police—retrospectively, this transition represented an important paradigm shift and the stepping-stone toward embracing the philosophy of community policing.

The principal focus of community policing was on building meaningful and collaborative partnerships with the community (Miller & Hess, 2005; Roberg et al., 2000). Because of the centrality accorded to the notion of *reconnecting with the community*, there have been multiple approaches and methodologies toward achieving the same goal while also underscoring the importance for improving recruitment, selection, and training. Addressing community policing, Miller and Hess (2005) suggest it consists of (a) building comprehensive partnerships between the police and the community, (b) collaborating in identifying and solving problems within the community, and (c) mitigating and preventing crime. Indisputably, its spirit and import have made significant strides toward bridging the many voids that have existed between the police and the community; however, not without the pains associated with the effects of the terrorist attack of September 11, 2001, which many contend resulted in a shift away from the philosophy of community policing and toward a fight against terrorism and protecting the homeland. Despite the public's initial support and sense of urgency as a result of the September 11 attacks, there has been a host of unintended consequences, which have included the real and perceived militarization of today's police.

POLICING CHALLENGES AND CURRENT STATE OF AFFAIRS

Complicating the emphasis placed on today's police for homeland security and the fight against terrorism, they also continue to be challenged with a complicated and integrated array of social, cultural, political, legal, economic, and technological changes. To be sure, the dichotomy of keeping society safe and secure while at the same time respecting and protecting citizens' constitutional rights can be a daunting task. Recent incidents involving the police and the tragic deaths of Michael Brown, Eric Garner, Tamir Rice, Walter Scott, and Freddie Gray[4] underscore the need to examine many of the issues that confront today's police and society. Addressing the concerns raised as a consequence of these tragedies (and what appears to many as a growing disconnect between the police and the communities they serve), President Barack Obama responded by stating that "when any part of the American family does not feel like it is being treated fairly, that's a problem for all of us." When that happens,

> it's not just a problem for some. It's not just a problem for a particular community or a particular demographic … it means that we are not as strong a country as we can be. And when applied to the criminal justice system, it means we're not as effective in fighting crime as we could be. (President's Task Force on 21st Century Policing, 2015)

And while these events surely speak to underlying issues and rightfully demand society's concern, investigation, and appropriate actions, it is equally important to point out that many diverse communities and their police enjoy excellent relationships.

Yet when looking at the police mission, *fighting crime* represents a relatively small part in maintaining social order and control. On average, less than 30% of police activities involve *fighting crime* such as making arrests for alleged violations of the law, while 70% of their time is spent on the many other social service activities. And while most arrests do not involve physical force and occur without incident, when they do result in injury—or even worse, death—their actions are rightfully scrutinized, both internally and externally. Indeed, as the country and the world has witnessed with the tragic deaths of Brown, Garner, Rice, Scott, and Gray, the impact of such incidents are exacerbated when they involve minority groups, accompanied

---

4   Michael Brown of Ferguson, Missouri; Eric Garner of New York City; Tamir Rice of Cleveland, Ohio; Walter Scott of North Charleston, South Carolina; and Freddie Gray of Baltimore, Maryland, were all African Americans who died during encounters with the police.

COPYRIGHTED MATERIAL — DO NOT DUPLICATE, DISTRIBUTE, OR POST

COPYRIGHTED MATERIAL — DO NOT DUPLICATE, DISTRIBUTE, OR POST

by accusations of bias, prejudice, discrimination, and excessive use of force.

While such incidents of late are undeniably tragic and rightfully called into question, they are all too often overshadowed by the many positive actions and contributions police make on a daily basis. While the media, including social media, play an important role in reporting the actions of the police—whether their actions may have been justified or not—it is equally important to acknowledge that some segments of the media play to their audiences, sensationalize, and exacerbate what has already been an inflamed and heart-wrenching set of events. Equally important, which Obama points to, are the deep-rooted causes that lead to criminality, over which the police have little or no control but by default are expected to address. While not to rationalize or justify criminal behavior, it is nevertheless important that today's police recognize and understand the causes and contributing factors of social unrest and criminal behavior, which all too often has its roots in a host of complex social, cultural, legal, political, economic, and historical issues. To be sure, there are endless and complex challenges that today's police confront on a daily basis, the majority of which are resolved amiably and without incident and hence are not newsworthy. However, it is when there is a breach of protocol and their actions violate their own rules and regulations, citizens' civil rights, and society's expectations for professionalism that their actions are rightfully called into question and come under intense scrutiny. While many such incidents reflect an escalation or a cataclysm of events that may or may not have been avoided, questions nevertheless arise whether better recruitment, selection, training, education, and institutional leadership could have resulted in different outcomes.

POLICE RECRUITMENT AND SELECTION

While many factors and variables play into the challenges that face today's police, not the least of which involve developing strategies to address the multitude of issues that contribute to the growing tensions between the police and community, there's the prospect that the *President's Task Force on 21st Century Policing* (2015) will lead to meaningful changes and reforms. Consistent with earlier police reforms, the area of police training and education has rightfully been identified as an important component to addressing the challenges that face today's police and society. An equally important and contingent area that serves as an antecedent to, and an integral component of, police training and education is the critical importance of recruitment and selection.

Building and developing a police force with individuals that possess the many qualifications needed to successfully perform the duties and responsibilities of a police officer, especially within today's society, is critically important. However, the ideal qualifications sought for police work may preclude otherwise qualified applicants from applying for the service. As most would agree, it is important to recruit and select prospective police officers that represent the communities they serve and society at large, irrespective of gender, culture, race, ethnicity, national origin, religion, or sexual orientation. Although an increasing number of policing agencies throughout the country have increased their outreach to attract and hire minority groups to include African American, Asian, Latino, Middle Eastern, and other underrepresented populations, doing so is proving difficult in many venues. This may be attributable to any number of factors that include culture, value systems, perceived status (or lack thereof), stigmatization, personal and community experiences and expectations, contempt for police and government, or simply not meeting the qualifications required for the position.

While many salient qualifications for police officers are considered to be universal and consist of standard criteria relative to age, citizenship, intelligence, aptitude, general knowledge, physical ability, a valid driver's license, and lack of a criminal conviction for an indictable offense, there are many other qualifications that should play a critical role in the recruitment and selection of police officers. For a host of reasons, however, many agencies do not set higher standards and procedures for recruiting and selecting candidates. Some of these include conducting exhaustive and comprehensive background investigations that can attest to a candidate's character and integrity, reputation, financial history

COPYRIGHTED MATERIAL — DO NOT DUPLICATE, DISTRIBUTE, OR POST

COPYRIGHTED MATERIAL — DO NOT DUPLICATE, DISTRIBUTE, OR POST

and responsibility, and academic records. Many also require comprehensive psychological testing, thorough medical and physical examinations to include drug testing and other screenings, multiple personal interviews, and the submission of writing samples. Undisputedly, perhaps most importantly, is ensuring a candidate's personal and professional integrity.

Similar to all federal law enforcement agencies, many argue that all police officers should be college educated given the sophistication of today's society and the many skill sets required of today's police (Carter, Sapp, & Stephens, 1988; Lumb, 1994; Roberg & Bonn, 2004). While most would agree that a college education in and of itself does not necessarily make for a better police officer, all things being equal, it can certainly be argued that a 4-year college (bachelor's) degree not only exposes students to the arts, sciences, humanities, and a host of other disciplines but, perhaps more importantly, provides them with a host of other learning experiences and opportunities (Polk & Armstrong, 2001). College provides students with the ability to develop critical-thinking and problem-solving skills, a greater understanding and appreciation of the strengths and opportunities that diversity offers, better communication and listening skills, tolerance, restraint, open-mindedness, and a greater degree of maturity. While a college education is by no means the panacea to addressing the ills of society and the challenges that police officers face in their commission for maintaining social order and control, one can certainly argue it is an important criterion, not unlike so many other professions in which a college degree serves as a prerequisite for employment. Even more importantly, notwithstanding the importance of many professions that require a college degree or some other advanced training and education, their duties and responsibilities do not involve the power and authority vested in police officers, including having to literally make life-and-death decisions.

THE CHALLENGE AND DICHOTOMY OF POLICE RECRUITMENT AND SELECTION

Notwithstanding the many arguments for requiring police officers to have attained a college education, the problem and challenge associated with establishing such criteria is that it may exclude otherwise qualified candidates. This raises a number of practical and ethical questions and concerns. Does increasing the qualifications, including possessing a college degree, limit the pool of applicants, particularly in some regions of the country and among minorities and the disenfranchised? Can requiring a college degree be considered discriminatory, given that not all segments of the population have equal access to the same educational opportunities? In the interest of acquiring greater diversity within police departments, should the standards for recruiting, selecting, and training police officers be changed or otherwise lowered? By not calling for greater qualifications in the selection and training of police officers, will the quality and caliber of professional policing be compromised, thus undermining their ability to effectively face the challenges as of late, which can further exacerbate the problems associated with developing better police–community relations? Conversely, will hiring greater numbers of underrepresented minority group police officers, without calling for greater qualifications, serve to mitigate much of the social unrest and violence that have marred the police and the communities they serve? Will the increase in qualifications and the remuneration that today's police receive, demand greater selectiveness in who is recruited and ultimately hired as a police officer? And lastly, given the unprecedented degree of scrutiny that today's police officers receive, in part as a result of an informed public and the impact of social media, will policing be challenged in its ability to attract and recruit qualified candidates?

POLICE TRAINING AND EDUCATION

While the mission of policing democratic societies has fundamentally remained unchanged over the course of the past 200 years, its role within society has undergone significant changes and transitions, as have the methods for achieving its goals and objectives (Roberg, Kuykendall, & Novak, 2002). Underscoring the challenges that today's police face is the importance of how new officers are trained and educated (Kappeler & Gaines, 2012; Walker &

COPYRIGHTED MATERIAL — DO NOT DUPLICATE, DISTRIBUTE, OR POST

COPYRIGHTED MATERIAL — DO NOT DUPLICATE, DISTRIBUTE, OR POST

Katz, 2005; Vodde, 2009). As with the issue of police recruitment and selection, police training and education in and of itself is not represented as the panacea for the innumerable challenges that face today's police. Nevertheless, the process represents a critical factor in the professional preparation of new police officers. While what Vodde (2009, p. 27) describes as a traditional, pedagogical, military model of training may have at one time served the needs and interests of society" (particularly given the emphasis of the *Reform Era of policing*), its applicability and efficacy have come under question and great scrutiny, especially considering what has been described as the militarization of today's police (Rizer, 2015). Toward that end, research suggests that an andragogical instructional methodology serves as a more effective means for training police recruits compared to the traditional, pedagogical, military model of training that still remains a mainstay within many, if not most, police academies throughout the United States.

Basic police training may be compared to the early imprinting and conditioning that occurs during a child's formative years. Holden (1994), underscoring the significance of police training and education, writes that "the most important process for ensuring organizational effectiveness is training," emphasizing that "the foundation of effective law enforcement is based on the quality of its training program" (pp. 279–281).

Addressing the goals and objectives of basic training, Vodde (2012) summarizes that it encompasses seven fundamental principles: (a) to orient an officer to the nature of police work, (b) to indoctrinate an officer with the organization and its goals and objectives, (c) to transfer the knowledge and skills necessary to perform the job, (d) to standardize procedures and increase efficiency, (e) to build confidence so that "critical tasks can be practiced and mastered in learning situations," (f) to enhance safety and help assure survival, and (g) to build morale and discipline (p. 323). Considering the foregoing, the mission of basic police training can be described as "a process to instill a recruit with the requisite knowledge, understanding, skills, attitudes, behaviors, and competencies necessary to efficiently and effectively discharge the duties and responsibilities inherent to that of a professional

police officer" (Vodde, 2012, p. 323). While such a mission may present itself as a straightforward "academic exercise," this is hardly the case, for the success of policing lies not just in *what* a police officer does but, perhaps more importantly, *how* one does it, which speaks to, in great part, the 6 months of *conditioning* that occurs during the process of basic training.

Toward those ends, an andragogical approach to police training and education—popular among a number of domestic and international police academies, most notably the Royal Canadian Mounted Police—represents a more user-friendly, holistic, integrative, and collaborative approach to basic police training and education. Its approach aligns with the philosophy of community policing and serves to meet the needs and demands of a changing society, including a new generation of police recruits, which now includes what has been labeled as *millennials* and *generation Z*. Andragogy is based on a set of assumptions about how adults learn versus that of how children learn, upon which traditional learning is based. It is rooted in the belief that adults learn differently than children and bases its practices on the needs, interests, readiness, orientation, experience, and motivation of the adult learner. Malcolm Knowles (1913–1997), revered by many as the *modern father of andragogy*, explains that his research into andragogy evolved not only from his growing understanding of pedagogy, but also from his ever-increasing knowledge about "adults as learners and their learning processes" (Knowles, 1990, p. 6). Framed in a collaborative context, learning involves problem-based exercises and assessments, simulations, the case method, and practical hands-on training exercises.

Not unlike the significance of police officers possessing college degrees, basic training for police officers is not represented as the panacea for the innumerable challenges that face today's police; however, it nevertheless plays a significant role in the formative years of a police officer's career. In many respects, basic police training leaves an indelible imprint that influences an officer's values, attitudes, understanding, and abilities (Bandura, 1977, 1997). In applying this methodology, recruits are immersed in a training program that

COPYRIGHTED MATERIAL — DO NOT DUPLICATE. DISTRIBUTE. OR POST

COPYRIGHTED MATERIAL — DO NOT DUPLICATE, DISTRIBUTE, OR POST

reflects a meaningful and insightful understanding of a training program's purpose, processes, and rationale; one that particularly provides an insight into understanding a changing society. This philosophy can represent for the recruit a belief and value system that serves as a compass and barometer throughout the training process. Further, the approach creates a physical and psychological climate that takes into consideration the affective needs of the recruit, thus providing for a healthy, engaging, challenging, and collaborative atmosphere in which recruits may develop a clear understanding and perspective of their role within the greater context of society. Underscoring the significance of these factors, an andragogical approach to training represents a well-planned and skillfully orchestrated process that holistically integrates all aspects of the curriculum.

Infused throughout the curriculum is the comprehensive use of multisensory, experiential, hands-on learning activities that allow recruits to apply what they have learned. This experiential component represents a synthesis of the cognitive, psychomotor, and affective components of the curriculum (Bloom, 1974). Lastly, given the physical and psychological challenges associated with all aspects of police training, stressful experiences and the need for discipline are skillfully integrated throughout all components of the curriculum as a means for assessing, preparing, and conditioning recruits' tolerance for stress and their capacity for appropriate response, whether cognitive, emotional, or physical. Further, while stress is also infused into self-directed activities that require self-discipline and control, the focus in these activities is on developing a positive attitude toward and accepting the responsibilities that accompany the specific activities and their real-life analogs. Stress and discipline, while demanding in their own right, are not perceived as punitively oriented or used in a derogatory context, but rather as an important and necessary element in the process toward reaching a clear and well-defined goal.

Summarily, studies and anecdotal evidence have revealed that an andragogical instructional methodology is an effective means for training police officers in that it serves the mutual needs and interests of the police recruit, the police organization, and society at large. It is a methodology in which recruits are equipped with the skill sets and competencies needed to meet the changing needs of a sophisticated, fast-paced, and ever-changing constituency.

CONCLUSION

Today's police officers must possess the ability to synthesize and pragmatically apply the innumerable academic disciplines addressed as part of their training curriculum, along with possessing a host of competencies in areas related to critical-thinking, decision-making, problem-solving, and effective communication skills; the latter includes the ability to deescalate volatile situations. These underscore the importance of not just *what* is learned during basic training but *how* and *why* it is learned. In effect, recruits must possess the ability not only to synthesize what has been learned but to pragmatically apply it within the field, highlighting the importance for developing a recruit's situational awareness, tactical vigilance, and the exercise of good judgment and discretion.

Collectively, the significance of recruiting, selecting, and training today's police officers presents a host of challenges, not only to the police but to all of society. Ensuring that today's police officers represent all segments of the communities they serve; that they possess the requisite integrity, qualifications, abilities, disposition, attitude, and understanding of the challenges inherent to serving and protecting society; and that they can acquire and maintain the necessary training, education, and skill sets to meet the ever-changing needs, interests, and demands of today's society represents a daunting challenge, yet nevertheless, an achievable goal when all the stakeholders recognize the critical role that they collectively share in providing for and maintaining social order and control within society at large.

COPYRIGHTED MATERIAL — DO NOT DUPLICATE, DISTRIBUTE, OR POST

COPYRIGHTED MATERIAL — DO NOT DUPLICATE, DISTRIBUTE, OR POST

Discussion Questions

1 Describe the eras of policing.
2 What is the militarization of policing?
3 Describe the andragogical approach to police training.
4 What role should police play in society?

REFERENCES

Ascoli, D. (1979). *The Queen's peace: The origins and development of the Metropolitan Police, 1829–1979*. London: Hamish Hamilton.

Bailey, W. G. (Ed.). (1995). *The encyclopedia of police science* (Vol. 1729). New York: Taylor & Francis.

Bandura, A. (1977). Self-efficacy: Toward a unifying theory of behavioral change. *Psychological Review, 84*(2), 191–215.

Bandura, A. (1997). *Self-efficacy: The exercise of control*. New York: Freeman.

Bloom, B. S. (1974). *Taxonomy of educational objectives: The classification of educational goals. Handbook 1–2.* New York: McKay.

Brandl, S. G., & Barlow, D. E. (Eds.). (2004). *The police in America: Classic and contemporary readings*. Belmont, CA: Wadsworth.

Carte, G. E., & Carte, E. H. (1975). *Police reform in the United States: The era of August Vollmer, 1905–1932.* Berkeley: University of California Press.

Carter, D. L., Sapp, A. D., & Stephens, D. W. (1988). Higher education as a bona fide occupational qualification (BFOQ) for police: A blueprint. *American Journal of Police, 7*(2), 1–27.

Champion, D. H., & Hooper, M. K. (2003). *Introduction to American policing*. New York: Glencoe/McGraw-Hill.

Friend, C. (2004). Social contract theory. In *Internet Encyclopedia of Philosophy*.

Gale, D. E. (1996). *Understanding urban unrest: From Reverend King to Rodney King*. Thousand Oaks, CA: Sage.

Holden, R. N. (1994). *Modern police management*. Upper Saddle River, NJ: Prentice Hall Career and Technology.

Kappeler, V. E., & Gaines, L. K. (2012). *Community policing: A contemporary perspective*. Abingdon, UK: Routledge.

Kelling, G. L., & Moore, M. H. (1998). The evolving strategy of policing. *Perspectives on Policing, 4*, 1–15. Washington, DC: National Institute of Justice.

Knowles, M. S. (1990). *The adult learner: A neglected species* (4th ed.). Houston, TX: Gulf.

Lumb, R. C. (1994). Standards of professionalization: Do the American police measure up? *Police Studies: The International Review of Police Development, 17*, 1–19.

Miller, L. S., & Hess, K. M. (2005). *Community policing: Partnerships for problem solving* (4th ed.). Belmont, CA: Thomson-Wadsworth.

Morris, C. W. (Ed.). (2000). *The social contract theorists: Critical essays on Hobbes, Locke, and Rousseau*. Lanham, MD: Rowman & Littlefield.

Polk, O. E., & Armstrong, D. A. (2001). Higher education and law enforcement career paths: Is the road to success paved by degree? *Journal of Criminal Justice Education, 12*(1), 77–99.

President's Task Force on 21st Century Policing. (2015). *Final report of the President's Task Force on 21st Century Policing*. Washington, DC: Office of Community Oriented Policing Services.

Riley, P. (1999). *Will and political legitimacy: A critical exposition of social contract theory in Hobbes, Locke, Rousseau, Kant, and Hegel*. Lincoln, NE: iUniverse.

Rizer, A. (2015). Trading police for soldiers: Has the Posse Comitatus Act helped militarize our police and set the stage for more Fergusons? *Nevada Law Journal, 16*(2), 467.

Roberg, R., & Bonn, S. (2004). Higher education and policing: Where are we now? *Policing: An International Journal of Police Strategies & Management, 27*(4), 469–486.

Roberg, R., Crank, J., & Kuykendall, J. (2000). *Police and society* (2nd ed.). Los Angeles: Roxbury.

COPYRIGHTED MATERIAL — DO NOT DUPLICATE. DISTRIBUTE. OR POST

COPYRIGHTED MATERIAL — DO NOT DUPLICATE, DISTRIBUTE, OR POST

Roberg, R. R., Kuykendall, J., & Novak, K. (2002) *Police management* (3rd ed.). Los Angeles: Roxbury.

Roberg, R., Novak, K., & Cordner, G. (2005). *Police and society* (3rd ed.). Los Angeles: Roxbury.

Schmalleger, F. J. (2015). *Criminology* (3rd ed.). Upper Saddle River, NJ: Prentice Hall.

Swanson, C. R., Territo, L., & Taylor, R. W. (2001) *Police administration: Structures, processes, and behavior* (5th ed.). Upper Saddle River, NJ: Prentice Hall.

Vodde, R. F. (2009). *Andragogical instruction for effective police training*. Amherst, NY: Cambria Press.

Vodde, R. F. (2012). Changing paradigms in police training: Transitioning from a traditional to an andragogical model. In M. R. Haberfeld, C. A. Clarke, & D. L. Sheehan (Eds.), *Police organization and training* (pp. 27–44). New York: Springer.

Walker, S., & Katz, C. M. (2005) *The police in America* (5th ed.). New York: McGraw-Hill.

Wickersham Report on Police. (1931). *The American Journal of Police Science, 2*(4), 337–348. doi:10.2307/1147362

COPYRIGHTED MATERIAL — DO NOT DUPLICATE. DISTRIBUTE. OR POST

COPYRIGHTED MATERIAL — DO NOT DUPLICATE, DISTRIBUTE, OR POST

2 | POLICE DISCRETION AND USE OF FORCE

EVELYN GARCIA, EdD

Reading Objectives

- Understand the democratic context of policing and the police role
- Understand the use of force continuum and its application in modern-day policing
- Identify ethical challenges and human rights issues associated with the use of force by police
- Recognize the need for greater control over police activities so that the potential for abuse can be curtailed

---

OVERVIEW

In the past year the media has been laden with images of unarmed African Americans being killed at the hands of police. These very unfortunate and highly controversial incidents have given way to speculation on the propriety of current police use-of-force practices. There are many questions that need to be answered, particularly whether these practices are outdated and in need of amending. The first section in this chapter examines the democratic context of policing, the role of police, and police use-of-force continuums. The second section examines the administrative and organizational challenges associated with police use of force, specifically the use of deadly force. The chapter concludes with recommendations for balancing public safety while ensuring the rights of all to liberty, equality, and justice.

DEMOCRATIC CONTEXT OF POLICING

In the United States there are approximately 1,000 law enforcement agencies. These agencies exist at the state and local levels. Although their jurisdictions and area of specializations may differ, their fundamental duties are strikingly similar—namely, to protect and serve. These agencies employ nearly 900,000 law enforcement officers who are authorized to make arrests and carry firearms (Bureau of Justice Statistics, 2008). In the United States "police officers are invested with a great deal of authority under a system of government in which authority is reluctantly granted and, when granted, sharply curtailed" (Goldstein, 1977, p. 1). Simply stated, this amounts to a tremendous amount of power. However, based on recent controversial police shootings, it is apparent that some officers use this authority wisely, but some may not.

ROLE OF THE POLICE

The role of the police is to protect and serve. They are charged with balancing their obligation to control crime while at the same time preserving individual civil liberties as outlined in the Bill of Rights. These rights serve to protect citizens against

13

COPYRIGHTED MATERIAL — DO NOT DUPLICATE, DISTRIBUTE, OR POST

COPYRIGHTED MATERIAL — DO NOT DUPLICATE, DISTRIBUTE, OR POST

abuses of police power. It is imperative that officers understand that in their pursuit of providing public safety, they must not abuse their authority. Officers should be aware of constitutional limits on police procedures. When there is disregard for these procedural protections, the relationship between the police and the community becomes uneasy.

DISCRETION

What is police discretion, and why is it so important, one might ask? Discretion is a legally recognized privilege granted to public functionaries (e.g., police officers) to make their own judgments and to act in an official capacity in situations or under conditions that are ambiguous, requiring a decision that is proper and just under the totality of the circumstances (Falcone, 2001). Simply stated, it is considered to be the opportunity for police officers to exercise choice in their enforcement activities. The way in which they exercise this discretion has the potential to result in grave consequences, making it an important theme to consider within the context of policing activities.

CONTROVERSIAL ISSUES

USE OF FORCE BY POLICE

Use of force by the police refers to "the amount of effort required by police to compel compliance by an unwilling subject" (International Association of Chiefs of Police, 2015). Most law enforcement agencies across the country have adapted a police use-of-force continuum, which describes several courses of action that may be taken to resolve a situation. These courses of action provide guidance on the amount of force that should be used by police when involved in encounters with the public. The logic behind the use-of-force continuum is that the officer is to match the level of suspect resistance with specific police tactics and weapons (Police Executive Research Forum, 2015). An example of a use-of-force continuum is provided in Table 2.1. When the level of force exceeds the level justifiable under the circumstances, the activities of the police come under public scrutiny. The use of force is controversial especially when its application is viewed as excessive. Yet local, state, and federal

TABLE 2.1 National Institute of Justice Use-of-Force Continuum

Officer presence: No force is used.
- Considered the best way to resolve a situation. The mere presence of a law enforcement officer works to deter a crime or defuse a situation. Officers' attitudes are professional and nonthreatening.

Verbalization: Force is not physical.
- Officers issue calm, nonthreatening commands, such as "Let me see your license and registration." Officers may increase their volume and shorten commands in an attempt to gain compliance. Short commands might include "Stop" or "Don't move."

Empty-hand control: Officers use bodily force to gain control of a situation.
- Soft technique. Officers use grabs, holds, and joint locks to restrain an individual.
- Hard technique. Officers use punches and kicks to restrain an individual.

Less lethal methods: Officers use less lethal technologies to gain control of a situation.
- Blunt impact. Officers may use a baton or projectile to immobilize a combative person.
- Chemical. Officers may use chemical sprays or projectiles embedded with chemicals to restrain an individual (e.g., pepper spray).
- Conducted energy devices (CEDs). Officers may use CEDs to immobilize an individual. CEDs discharge a high-voltage, low-amperage jolt of electricity at a distance.

Lethal force: Officers use lethal weapons to gain control of a situation. Should only be used if a suspect poses a serious threat to an officer or another individual.
- Officers use deadly weapons such as firearms to stop an individual's actions.

Source: https://www.nij.gov/topics/law-enforcement/officer-safety/use-of-force/Pages/continuum.aspx.

COPYRIGHTED MATERIAL — DO NOT DUPLICATE. DISTRIBUTE. OR POST

COPYRIGHTED MATERIAL — DO NOT DUPLICATE, DISTRIBUTE, OR POST

governments actually collect and report very little information about police use of force, much less than about police behavior in general.

ETHICAL CHALLENGES AND HUMAN RIGHTS ISSUES

It was determined that 40 million persons had contact with the police during 2008 (Reaves, 2011). Of those 40 million contacted respondents, an estimated 776,000 (1.9%) reported the use of force at least once during these contacts. It has been established that only a small percentage of police public contact results in death. However, from 2003 to 2009, a total of 4,813 arrest-related deaths were reported. Of that number, 2,931, or about 6 of 10 deaths, were classified as homicide by law enforcement personnel. Whites accounted for 42% of reported arrest-related deaths, 32% were African American, and 20% were Hispanic (U.S. Department of Justice, 2011). According to the numbers presented, it might appear that a relatively small number (less than .003%) of the cases of reported use of force were classified as homicide by law enforcement personnel. These numbers are consistent with the extant research on excessive force, which suggests that it is rarely used (Alpert & Dunham, 1997; Alpert et al., 2001; Alpert & Smith, 1999; Durose & Eith, 2011; Henriquez, 2001). To the untrained observer, these statistics may appear to be of no consequence; however, attention needs to be paid to the details.

The research value of Uniform Crime Reports is questionable in terms of the actual accounts of homicide by police, because a significant amount of the incidences are not reported. Police reports to the FBI are voluntary and vary in accuracy. Researchers basically have to rely on victimization data and self-report studies in order to determine whether the subjects had been victimized. Currently, victimization by police is not a category reflected in National Crime Victimization Surveys.

The following is a summary of the article "Toward a National Estimate of Police Use of Nonlethal Force," by Matthew J. Hickman, Alex R. Piquero, and Joel H. Garner (2008).

LACK OF NATIONAL POLICING STANDARDS

The lack of national policing standards on police use of force has been a point of contention for many academics, police managers, and particularly law enforcement reform advocates. This lack of standards makes it challenging to uncover the extent of and the motives behind such use of force. In 2008, Hickman et al. (2008) identified 36 publications that report an incident-based rate of force. They were able to identify the sources of data used, types of situations studied, jurisdictions included in the research, and the dates of data collection. Six sources of data to estimate the amount of force use on the public by police were identified: arrest reports, household surveys, independent observations, police surveys, suspect surveys, and use-of-force forms. Nearly half (15 of 36) of the publications are based on independent observations of the police; 10 are based on surveys of police officers or arrested suspects; 8 derive data from official police use-of-force forms; and 3 use household surveys.

So the lack of consistent and reliable national-level data on police use of force is one of the most severe criticisms of this entire body of research and a continuing theme in research on both lethal and nonlethal use of force. Researchers (Adams, 1995; Alpert & Fridell, 1992; Fyfe, 1988; Geller & Scott, 1992; Geller & Toch, 1995; Klockars, 1995; Matulia, 1982; Pate & Fridell, 1993, 1995; Sherman & Langworthy, 1979) and big-city police chiefs (James, 1991), as well as law enforcement reform advocates (*Crime Control Digest*, 1991), have called for expanded databases at both the local and national levels on all uses of force, not just lethal force.

COPYRIGHTED MATERIAL — DO NOT DUPLICATE, DISTRIBUTE, OR POST

COPYRIGHTED MATERIAL — DO NOT DUPLICATE, DISTRIBUTE, OR POST

This is where the ethical issue arises, given the nature of how and the rate at which use-of-force data is collected; the latent abuse of deadly force by the police on unarmed young African American males goes unexposed. Police agencies are not holding their representatives accountable for their actions. In the early 1990s Pate and Fridell (1993) explored the scope and depth of existing requirements for reporting use of force within individual law enforcement agencies, as a basis for a national reporting system. Calls for a national reporting system were enhanced with the 1994 Violent Crime Control and Law Enforcement Act's provisions calling on the U.S. attorney general to "acquire data about the use of excessive force by law enforcement officers" and to "publish an annual summary of the data."

Unfortunately, Congress has provided no funds to support this mandate, and the U.S. Department of Justice has issued no annual summaries of national-level data about police use of force, excessive or otherwise. With regard to the use of lethal force, Fyfe (2002) asserts that it is shameful that "we still live in a society in which the best data on police use of force come to us not from the government or from scholars, but from the *Washington Post*" (p. 99). Kane (2007) argues that departments should adopt data collection and dissemination not for research purposes but as a professional standard for policing.

JUSTIFYING THE USE OF DEADLY FORCE

Although current available data sets provide us with a general idea of the nature of these deadly encounters, they do not provide indicators of whether these uses of deadly force by the police are justified. The extent to which the police use (and misuse) their authority to inflict physical force is a persistent controversy in criminology.

Researchers have developed a way to gauge and assess use-of-force incidents (Alpert & Dunham, 1997; Alpert et al., 2001; Terrill, Leinfelt, & Dae-Hoon, 2008). They developed instruments that assess relative degrees of force in relation to citizen resistance. They argued that one must measure suspects' levels of resistance and officers' levels of resistance both on the same scale. Using the highest level of resistance and force within an individual incident, the force factor is calculated by subtracting the level of resistance from the level of force (force—resistance = force factor). If the level of force is higher than the level of resistance, then the force factor is positive, with 1 point for each level of incongruence. Agencies that adopt the force factor approach will learn about their officers, supervisors, and encounters with the public they serve.

TABLE 2.2 Force Factor

Resistance levels	Officer force levels
1. Cooperative and/or no resistance	1. Police presence and/or verbal direction
2. Verbal noncompliance, passive resistance, and/or psychological intimidation	2. Strong verbal order (minimal contact)
3. Defensive resistance and/or attempted to flee	3. Forcibly subdued—hands or feet (defensive use—open hand or oleoresin capsicum spray)
4. Active resistance	4. Forcibly subdued—hands or feet (offensive use—open hand)

COPYRIGHTED MATERIAL — DO NOT DUPLICATE, DISTRIBUTE, OR POST

COPYRIGHTED MATERIAL — DO NOT DUPLICATE, DISTRIBUTE, OR POST

Resistance levels	Officer force levels
5. Aggravated active resistance	5. Forcibly subdued—intermediate weapon (used weapon—nondeadly)
6. Active resistance (with a deadly weapon)	6. Deadly force

Understanding the context in which these encounters occur will aid in developing comprehensive law enforcement reform. Sadly, in the recent deaths of Eric Garner, Michael Brown, Tamir Rice, and Walter Scott (to name a few), it seems as though there were ways that the police could have avoided the unnecessary use of deadly force.

Extant research has documented variations in subject characteristics and the use of force. For instance, ethnic/racial minorities are more likely to have force used against them than are Whites, younger individuals are more likely to have force used against them than are older individuals, and males are involved in use-of-force situations more frequently than are females (Hickman et al., 2008). To a lesser extent, prior research has also found a connection between some officer-based characteristics such as officer sex, race, experience, and educational levels (Worden, 1995).

Despite long-standing support for the collection and reporting of national-level data on police use of force, the existing research literature—although extensive and informative for other purposes—does not provide a reasonable basis for estimating either the amount of force used by police in the United States or the correlates of force.

CONCLUSION

It is important that, despite the fact that much of the data on police use of deadly force is not disclosed, we urge all state attorneys general to enhance the collection and disclosure of data on fatalities involving the police. Additionally, police department administrators should be held accountable when officers under their command engage in such practices. One way to hold police departments accountable is by requiring leadership to submit a plan of action outlining how they as an organization plan to address these breaches of conduct. This type of mandate would force the organizations to take a proactive approach to combat the use of all types of force, including deadly force, thereby promoting a culture among police managers in which they constantly reflect on where they are as an organization in both the now and in the future.

It is important to understand that before one can begin to judge the appropriateness of police use of force, one should measure and consider the extent to which force is applied proportionately and incrementally. Although these processes are fairly complex and may be difficult to implement, it will provide important information to agencies and the public, both of whom have a vested interest.

Once these illogical displays of force have been identified, it is up to police officials to develop the appropriate training for their members. In O'Keefe's 2003 work on police training, he offers sound and practical advice on how to prepare trainees for policing in the 21st century. The bigger question becomes, where does the training actually begin? In the landscape of American higher education, there are numerous criminal justice programs that prepare prospective law enforcement candidates. Perhaps the quality and content of those programs require an examination as well.

COPYRIGHTED MATERIAL — DO NOT DUPLICATE, DISTRIBUTE, OR POST

COPYRIGHTED MATERIAL — DO NOT DUPLICATE, DISTRIBUTE, OR POST

Discussion Questions

1   Why is it important to establish national policing standards?

2   What are the sources of possible ethical dilemmas associated with current use-of-force practices employed by police officers?

3   How can "force factor" models help police mangers develop effective use-of-force policies for police officers?

REFERENCES

Adams, K. (1995). Measuring the prevalence of police abuse of force. In W. A. Geller & H. Toch (Eds.), *And justice for all: Understanding and forum* (pp. 61–98). Washington, DC: Police Executive Research Forum.

Alpert, G. P., & Dunham, R. G. (1997). *The force factor: Measuring police use of force relative to suspect resistance.* Washington, DC: Police Executive Research Forum.

Alpert, G. P., Dunham, R. G., Smith, M., Kenney, D., Madden, T., & Terril, W. (2001). *The force factor: Measuring police use of force relative to suspect resistance.* Washington, DC: US Department of Justice.

Alpert, G., & Fridell, L. (1992). *Police vehicles and firearms: Instruments of deadly force.* Prospect Heights, IL: Waveland Press.

Alpert, G. P., & Smith, M. R. (1999). Police use of force data: Where we are and where we should be going. *Police Quarterly, 2,* 57–78.

Bureau of Justice Statistics. (2008). *Census of state and local law enforcement agencies, 2008* (NCJ 233982). Retrieved from https://www.bjs.gov/content/pub/pdf/csllea08.pdf

Crime Control Digest. (1991). AELE [Americans for Effective Crime Control] calls for national reporting system on use of force, police misconduct. *Crime Control Digest, 1,* 1.

Durose, M., & Eith, C. (2011). *Contacts between police and the public declined from 2002 to 2008.* Washington, DC: Government Printing Office.

Falcone, D. N. (2001). The Missouri Highway Patrol as a representative model. *Policing: An International Journal of Police Strategies and Management, 24,* 585–594.

Fyfe, J. (1988). Police use of deadly force: Research and reform. *Justice Quarterly, 5,* 165–207.

Fyfe, J. (2002). Too many missing cases: Holes in our knowledge about police use of force. *Justice Research and Policy, 4,* 87–102.

Geller, W., & Scott, M. (1992). *Deadly force: What we know.* Washington, DC: Police Executive Research Forum.

Geller, W., & Toch, H. (1995). Improving our understanding and control of police abuse of force: Recommendations for research and action. In W. A. Geller & H. Toch (Eds.), *And justice for all: Understanding and controlling police abuse of force* (pp. 277–338). Washington, DC: Police Executive Research Forum.

Goldstein, H. (1977). *Policing a free society.* Cambridge, MA: Ballinger.

Henriquez, M. (2001). *Police use of force in America.* Alexandria, VA: International Association of Chiefs of Police.

Hickman, M. J., Piquero, A. R., & Garner, J. H. (2008). Toward a national estimate of police use of nonlethal force. *Criminology & Public Policy, 7*(4), 563–603.

International Association of Chiefs of Police. (2015). *Use of force model policy.* Retrieved from http://www.theiacp.org/Portals/0/pdfs/Publications/2001useofforce.pdf

James, G. (1991, April 17). Police chiefs call for U.S. system to gather data on excessive force. *New York Times,* p. A2.

Kane, R. (2007). Collect and release data on coercive police actions. *Criminology & Public Policy, 6,* 773–780.

Klockars, C. (1995). A theory of excessive force and its control. In W. A. Geller & H. Toch (Eds.), *And justice for all: Understanding and controlling police abuse of force* (pp. 11–30). Washington, DC: Police Executive Research Forum.

Matulia, K. (1982). *A balance of forces: A study of justifiable homicides by the police.* Gaithersburg, MD: International Association of Chiefs of Police.

O'Keefe, J. (2003). *Protecting the republic: The education and training of American police officers.* Upper Saddle River, NJ: Prentice Hall.

COPYRIGHTED MATERIAL — DO NOT DUPLICATE. DISTRIBUTE. OR POST

COPYRIGHTED MATERIAL — DO NOT DUPLICATE, DISTRIBUTE, OR POST

Pate, A., & Fridell, L. (1993). *Police use of force: Official reports, citizen complaints, and legal consequences.* Washington, DC: Police Foundation.

Pate, A., & Fridell, L. (1995). Toward the uniform reporting of police use of force: Results of a national survey. *Criminal Justice Review, 20,* 123–145.

Police Executive Research Forum. (2015). *Critical issues in policing series: Re-engineering training on police use of force.* Retrieved from http://www.policeforum.org/assets/reengineeringtraining1.pdf

Reaves, B. (2011). *Census of state and local law enforcement agencies.* Washington, DC: Bureau of Justice Statistics.

Sherman, L., & Langworthy, R. (1979). Measuring homicide by police officers. *Journal of Criminal Law and Criminology, 70,* 546–560.

Terrill, W., Leinfelt, F. H., & Dae-Hoon, K. (2008). Examining police use of force: A smaller agency perspective. *Policing, 31*(1), 57–76.

US Department of Justice, Office of Justice Programs, Bureau of Justice Statistics. (2011). Police-public contact survey, Ann Arbor, MI: Inter-university Consortium for Political and Social Research [distributor], 2014-03-18. Retrieved from https://doi.org/10.3886/ICPSR34276.v1

Worden, R. (1995). The "causes" of police brutality: Theory and evidence on police use of force. In W. A. Geller & H. Toch (Eds.), *And justice for all: Understanding and controlling police abuse of force* (pp. 31–60). Washington, DC: Police Executive Research Forum.

COPYRIGHTED MATERIAL — DO NOT DUPLICATE. DISTRIBUTE. OR POST

COPYRIGHTED MATERIAL — DO NOT DUPLICATE, DISTRIBUTE, OR POST

COPYRIGHTED MATERIAL — DO NOT DUPLICATE. DISTRIBUTE. OR POST

COPYRIGHTED MATERIAL — DO NOT DUPLICATE, DISTRIBUTE, OR POST

3 | COMMUNITY AND POLICE RELATIONS

Reading Objectives

- Understand the characteristics of community trust and partnership and their influence on 21st-century policing
- Recognize and apply strategies to develop stronger relations between the community and the police

---

OVERVIEW

The quality of any relationship can be measured by whether involved parties respect each other and share a mutual trust. Lack of either could lead to strained relations. This same logic can be applied to the case of community–police relations in the United States; if there is a lack of respect or mutual trust, relations are strained. In modern-day policing, there is the potential for these strained relations to result in displays of civil unrest and other rather unfortunate incidences; namely, death. Recent events such as the death of Freddy Grey, who on April 19, 2015, died while in police custody in Baltimore, Maryland; the death of Tamir Rice; a 12-year-old boy who was shot by police officers in Cleveland, Ohio, on November 22, 2014; the shooting of Michael Brown by police on August 9, 2014, in Ferguson, Missouri; the death of Sandra Bland, who was found hanged in a jail cell while in police custody in Waller County, Texas, on July 13, 2014; and the release of the U.S. Department of Justice Report on Ferguson, Missouri, all serve as examples of the culmination of rising tensions between the community and police. These are just recent examples; there are many other incidents that raise the questions regarding police use of force.

As discussed in Chapter 2, police use-of-force continuums prescribe that an officer's use of force should be commensurate with the amount of force being used on them. When the use of force is considered to be unjustified, many, particularly those affected, question police practices and their legitimacy. In this chapter the literature on community–police relations will be reviewed to provide context to the issue, as well as strategies to strengthen these fragmented relationships.

PUBLIC PERCEPTION OF THE POLICE

In a democratic society, public opinion of criminal justice systems is essential for the proper functioning of police departments. Since the 1970s, police organizations were increasingly concerned with their relations with the public. Early researchers found that overall, Americans were generally satisfied with police services (Apple & O'Brien, 1983; Black, 1970, 1984; Brooks, 1993; Huang &

21

COPYRIGHTED MATERIAL — DO NOT DUPLICATE, DISTRIBUTE, OR POST

COPYRIGHTED MATERIAL — DO NOT DUPLICATE, DISTRIBUTE, OR POST

Vaughn, 1996; Thomas & Hyman, 1977; Zamble & Annesley, 1987). These early studies found that minority citizens viewed the police in a more negative way than White citizens. To date, this is a recurring theme in the public perception of the police research.

COMMUNITIES OF DISTINCTION— PERCEPTION OF POLICE

More recent research on public attitudes toward the police uses various proxies by which to examine the origins of such sentiments. Proxies used to measure the factors said to influence public attitudes toward the police are derived from demographics, neighborhood context, police–citizen interaction (Lai & Zhao, 2010), and ethnic identity (Lee, Steinberg, & Piquero; 2010). Additionally, there is a body of research on community–police perceptions that provides a framework for race and how it impacts attitudes about the police and shapes police–citizen interactions (Dunham & Alpert, 1988; Eitle, D'Alessio, & Stolzenberg, 2002; Lundman & Kaufman, 2003; MacDonald & Shildrick, 2007; Reisig & Parks, 2000; Stolzenberg, D'Alessio, & Eitle, 2004; Weitzer & Tuch, 1999).

Researchers have provided empirical evidence of the effects of race on public perceptions of and encounters with police. It is found that Blacks are less likely than Whites and Latinos to have confidence in the police and are more likely than these groups to report that they have had negative encounters with the police (Russell-Brown, 2009; Hendricks, Kelley, Gordon, & Foley, 2015). There is very little research that examines police–suspect contacts from the perspective of the suspect.

In 2006 Brunson and Miller examined 40 young men's experiences with and perceptions of police harassment and misconduct. They found that both adult and juvenile African American males in the United States report more dissatisfaction with and distrust for the police than any other group. They found that most respondents reported being harassed and disrespected. The participants reported being subjected to verbal abuse, which involved derogatory comments, name-calling, and offensive language. What was interesting to note is that although this kind of behavior is difficult for police administrators to identify and control, it has a tremendous impact on the perception of police by these young men.

Yet another approach taken by researchers to understand the underlying discourse between the police and community is to take police behavior into account when examining citizen and police encounters. A positive correlation was found between the officers' initial approach to their intended suspect and the intended subject's subsequent response. Namely, that as the level of aggression or disrespect on behalf of the officer increased, the likelihood of being met with resistance or noncompliance increased as well (Mastrofski, Snipes, & Supina, 1996; Terrill & Reisig, 2003). Mastrofski, Reisig, and McCluskey (2002) reported that negative police actions such as disrespect occur more frequently in disadvantaged urban communities with young African American males. These findings suggest that police officer demeanor complicates interaction with members of poor minority communities.

There is literature that points to the racial composition of the neighborhood as a framework by which to understand community–police relations. Heterogeneous neighborhoods are considered unique social contexts within which racial prejudice is likely to flourish and in which Blacks are likely to experience the greatest levels of discrimination from the police and others (Black, 1970; Blau, 1977). As Blau (1977) points out, contact among different racial groups is likely to be maximized in racially heterogeneous areas.

In 2011 Gabbidon, Higgins, and Potter examined the experiences of African Americans who believed that they had been recently treated unfairly by the police. They were particularly interested in whether gender affects perception of unfair treatment by the police. They found that African American women residing in the South were less likely to report unfair treatment by the police. For African American women, they found that being older and reporting higher levels of income is negatively correlated with the perception of having being treated unfairly by the police.

Researchers have also found that reported experiences with racial discrimination are associated with a variety of adverse consequences for Blacks, which include lower levels of self-esteem

COPYRIGHTED MATERIAL — DO NOT DUPLICATE, DISTRIBUTE, OR POST

COPYRIGHTED MATERIAL — DO NOT DUPLICATE, DISTRIBUTE, OR POST

and perceived social support, weaker academic commitment and performance, higher levels of depression, gang involvement, delinquency, and other problems (Kessler, Mickelson, & Williams, 1999; Neblett, Philip, Cogburn, & Sellers, 2006; Prelow, Mosher, & Bowman, 2006; Simons & Burt, 2011; Simons & Simons, 2006; Simons, Stewart, Gordon, & Conger, 2002). These effects have the potential to ruin lives and entire communities.

POLICE PERCEPTION OF COMMUNITY

Conceptions of procedural justice—that police organizations demonstrate to the public they serve that they are fair and impartial in the administration of justice—are often examined from the public's point of view. This approach seems logical, given that it is the civilian's perception that will influence perceptions of legitimacy, and in turn their willingness to cooperate with the police (Jonathan-Zamir, Mastrofski, & Moyal, 2013; Tankebe, 2009). However, considerably less is known about how police perceive their own interactions with the public. In order to get a more complete picture of community–police relations, research from the perspective of the police officer should be examined as well.

There is research that examines police attitudes and perceptions and their impact on various aspects on police behavior; however, this research tends to focus on factors that influence policing behaviors (Wells & Schafer, 2006) or differences in police views based on factors such as gender (Homant & Kennedy, 1985).

In 2005 Jackson and Wade took a sociological approach to understanding whether a relationship existed between social capital (as a proxy for community context) and police sense of responsibility to engage in proactive policing. Social capital is an asset, embedded in social relations, that can be used to improve one's life outcomes. It includes norms and information channels available through relationships with others (Coleman, 1988; Lin, 2000).

For analytical clarity, social capital refers to the instrumental or supportive relationships with two types of "agents." Institutional agents refer to those individuals who have the capacity and commitment to transmit directly, or negotiate the transmission of institutional resources and opportunities. Institutional agents would include professionals in the criminal justice system; that is, law enforcement personnel. Protective agents refer to the relations embodied in family and community-based networks; for example, parents, grandparents, other relatives, caring neighbors, and prosocial peers (Stanton-Salazar, 1997).

Through relationships with institutional agents, individuals are able to gain access to resources, privileges, and support necessary to advance and maintain their economic position in society. Community social capital in the literature has been identified as having a significant impact on police behavior mainly because social capital serves as a measure of the community's ability to solve its own problems. In communities with low social capital, police may perceive themselves as the only form of social order and may therefore develop a higher sense of responsibility toward protecting citizens, themselves, and preventing crime.

Jackson and Wade (2005) also assessed the impact of a sense of responsibility on their tendency to engage in proactive policing. A three-item social scale was developed, and respondents were asked questions that focused on the community's ability to solve problems and plan for the future, as well as economic prospects in the future. Proactive policing is considered discretionary behavior that involves actions such as stop and frisk, ignoring minor crimes, removing prostitutes, dealing with citizen loitering, asking for identification, and removing drunks. By examining police perceptions of social capital and their sense of responsibility, it is possible to understand police behavior in environments that by their structural and demographic composition complicate the task of effective policing. Jackson and Wade found that the quality of the social networks was correlated to both the officers' sense of responsibility and proactive policing. Namely, that as the quality of the networks decreased, there was a demonstrative increase in the both the officers' sense of responsibility and proactive policing.

While examining police behavior, it is equally important to understand that the role of the police means that they interact with citizens when they are most vulnerable; they must contend with

COPYRIGHTED MATERIAL — DO NOT DUPLICATE, DISTRIBUTE, OR POST

COPYRIGHTED MATERIAL — DO NOT DUPLICATE, DISTRIBUTE, OR POST

stressful and volatile situations and may have to take actions that every individual involved is unlikely to view positively. The uncertainty associated with police–citizen interactions also challenges the relationship from the police point of view: although officers interacting with citizens courteously and respectfully are critically important, they must do so with the knowledge that seemingly routine interactions could escalate into threats to their or others' safety.

Confidence in the police and police legitimacy are essential elements in police–community relations. Research shows that individuals who trust in and have had positive encounters with the police are more likely to be satisfied with law enforcement and reach out to them in times of need. Community members are also more likely to cooperate with police when information is needed and work together to solve community problems (Hinds & Murphy, 2007; Tyler & Wakslak, 2004). The relationship between the police and the community that they serve and protect is important, and building and maintaining police–community trust is challenging.

IMPROVING COMMUNITY PUBLIC RELATIONS

Recent events, including the deaths of citizens as a result of police use of force and targeted killings of police officers in the line of duty, illustrate that there is a need to focus national attention on the relationship between the police and the public they serve. Many communities across the country have strong and productive relationships with the law enforcement agencies that serve them. However, in minority or economically disadvantaged neighborhoods this does not appear to be the case. Clearly, tensions exist, and in order to move forward, the trust between the two needs to be strengthened. To trust and respect is a two-way street, and both sides must be willing to travel the path.

TRANSPARENCY AND POLICE–COMMUNITY TRUST

Strengthening trust between police and the community has been at the forefront of discussion among police administrators. At a 2015 policy summit on community–police relations convened by the International Association of Chiefs of Police, participants identified communication, partnership, and trust as conceptual elements of strong community–police relations. It was suggested that law enforcement agencies improve communication, understanding, education, and transparency in order to create a culture of trust and inclusion and improve community–police relationships. In its report, the International Association of Chiefs of Police provided a comprehensive listing of recommended action steps for both law enforcement agencies and stakeholders.

CONCLUSION

When displays of civil unrest such as those that began in Ferguson, Missouri, during the summer of 2014 are examined, it is evident that the protests that have unfolded there are not simply about unfair policing in that town; rather, they are the result of a deep and broad collection of official decisions that residents, not surprisingly, interpret as demeaning to them. During the race riots of the 1960s, the Kerner Commission, charged with investigating urban unrest, hypothesized that conditions in slum living such as poor housing, schools, and jobs fueled the violent reactions of residents, but the reporters also fingered tensions between police and residents of so-called racial ghettos as a prime cause of *every* riot during the period. The commission noted specifically that public confrontations between law enforcement personnel and residents of segregated urban neighborhoods, usually ordinary arrests or stops as opposed to extraordinary and tragic events like the one in Ferguson, specifically sparked many riots. Policing incidents may trigger social unrest, but the true causes are much deeper and broader.

COPYRIGHTED MATERIAL — DO NOT DUPLICATE, DISTRIBUTE, OR POST

COPYRIGHTED MATERIAL — DO NOT DUPLICATE, DISTRIBUTE, OR POST

Discussion Questions

1 What role do community–police relations play in regard to the administration of justice?

2 How can police protect themselves and others while building relationships with their communities, particularly those who feel mistreated or misunderstood by police?

3 Can there be vigilance without fear and bias?

4 Can community trust be built while decreasing crime rates?

REFERENCES

Apple, N., & O'Brien, D. J. (1983). Neighborhood racial composition and residents' evaluation of police performance. *Journal of Police Science and Administration, 11*(1), 76–84.

Black, D. J. (1970). Production of crime rates. *American Sociological Review,* 733–748.

Black, D. (1984). Social control as a dependent variable. *Toward a General Theory of Social Control, 1,* 1–36.

Blau, P. M. (1977). A macrosociological theory of social structure. *American Journal of Sociology, 83*(1), 26–54.

Brooks, L. W. (1993). Police discretionary behavior. *Critical Issues in Policing: Contemporary Readings,* 140–164.

Brunson, R. K., & Miller, J. (2006). Gender, race, and urban policing: The experience of African American youths. *Gender & Society, 20*(4), 531–552.

Coleman, J. S. (1988). Social capital in the creation of human capital. *American Journal of Sociology, 94,* S95–S120.

Dunham, R. G., & Alpert, G. P. (1988). Neighborhood differences in attitudes toward policing: Evidence for a mixed-strategy model of policing in a multi-ethnic setting. *Journal of Criminal Law and Criminology, 79*(2), 504–523.

Eitle, D., D'Alessio, S. J., & Stolzenberg, L. (2002). Racial threat and social control: A test of the political, economic, and threat of Black crime hypotheses. *Social Forces, 81*(2), 557–576.

Gabbidon, S. L., Higgins, G. E., & Potter, H. (2011). Race, gender, and the perception of recently experiencing unfair treatment by the police: Exploratory results from an all-Black sample. *Criminal Justice Review, 36*(1), 5–21.

Hendricks, A., Kelley, J., Gordon, P., & Foley, A. (2015). *Citizen perceptions of police in the post-Ferguson era: A survey in partnership with the Richmond County Sheriff's Office.* Retrieved from augusta.openrepository.com

Hinds, L., & Murphy, K. (2007). Public satisfaction with police: Using procedural justice to improve police legitimacy. *Australian & New Zealand Journal of Criminology, 40*(1), 27–42.

Homant, R. J., & Kennedy, D. B. (1985). Police perceptions of spouse abuse: A comparison of male and female officers. *Journal of Criminal Justice, 13*(1), 29–47.

Huang, W., & Vaughn, M. S. (1996). Support and confidence: Public attitudes toward the police. In T. J. Flanagan & D. R. Longmire (Eds.), *Americans view crime and justice: A national public opinion survey* (pp. 31–45). Thousand Oaks, CA: Sage.

International Association of Chiefs of Police. (2015). *National Policy Summit on Community Police Relations: Advancing a culture of community trust.* Alexandria, VA: Author.

Jackson, A. L., & Wade, J. E. (2005). Police perceptions of social capital and sense of responsibility: An explanation of proactive policing. *Policing: An International Journal of Police Strategies & Management, 28*(1), 49–68.

Jonathan-Zamir, T., Mastrofski, S. D., & Moyal, S. (2013). Measuring procedural justice in police–citizen encounters. *Justice Quarterly.* Advance online publication.. doi: 10.1080/07418825.2013.845677

Kessler, R. C., Mickelson, K. D., & Williams, D. R. (1999). The prevalence, distribution, and mental health correlates of perceived discrimination in the United States. *Journal of Health and Social Behavior, 40*(3), 208–230.

Lai, Y. L., & Zhao, J. S. (2010). The impact of race/ethnicity, neighborhood context, and police/citizen interaction on residents' attitudes toward the police. *Journal of Criminal Justice, 38*(4), 685–692.

COPYRIGHTED MATERIAL — DO NOT DUPLICATE. DISTRIBUTE. OR POST

COPYRIGHTED MATERIAL — DO NOT DUPLICATE, DISTRIBUTE, OR POST

Lee, J. M., Steinberg, L., & Piquero, A. R. (2010). Ethnic identity and attitudes toward the police among African American juvenile offenders. *Journal of Criminal Justice, 38*(4), 781–789.

Lin, N. (2000). Inequality in social capital. *Contemporary Sociology, 29*(6), 785–795.

Lundman, R. J., & Kaufman, R. L. (2003). Driving while Black: Effects of race, ethnicity, and gender on citizen self-reports of traffic stops and police actions. *Criminology, 41*, 195.

MacDonald, R., & Shildrick, T. (2007). Street corner society: Leisure careers, youth (sub) culture and social exclusion. *Leisure Studies, 26*(3), 339–355.

Mastrofski, S. D., Reisig, M. D., & McCluskey, J. D. (2002). Police disrespect toward the public: An encounter based analysis. *Criminology, 40*(3), 519–552.

Mastrofski, S. D., Snipes, J. B., & Supina, A. E. (1996). Compliance on demand: The public's response to specific police requests. *Journal of Research in Crime and Delinquency, 33*(3), 269–305.

Neblett, E. W., Philip, C. L., Cogburn, C. D., & Sellers, R. M. (2006). African American adolescents' discrimination experiences and academic achievement: Racial socialization as a cultural compensatory and protective factor. *Journal of Black Psychology, 32*(2), 199–218.

Prelow, H. M., Mosher, C. E., & Bowman, M. A. (2006). Perceived racial discrimination, social support, and psychological adjustment among African American college students. *Journal of Black Psychology, 32*(4), 442–454.

Reisig, M. D., & Parks, R. B. (2000). Experience, quality of life, and neighborhood context: A hierarchical analysis of satisfaction with police. *Justice Quarterly, 17*(3), 607–630.

Russell-Brown, K. (2009). *The color of crime.* New York: New York University Press.

Simons, R. L., & Burt, C. H. (2011). Learning to be bad: Adverse social conditions, social schemas, and crime. *Criminology, 49*(2), 553–598.

Simons, R. L., & Simons, L. G. (2006). A longitudinal test of the effects of parenting and the stability of self-control: Negative evidence for the general theory of crime. *Criminology, 44*(2), 353–396.

Simons, R. L., Stewart, E., Gordon, L. C., & Conger, R. D. Jr. (2002). A test of life-course explanations for stability and change in antisocial behavior from adolescence to young adulthood. *Criminology, 40*(2), 401–434.

Stanton-Salazar, R. (1997). A social capital framework for understanding the socialization of racial minority children and youths. *Harvard Educational Review, 67*(1), 1–41.

Stolzenberg, L., D'Alessio, S. J., & Eitle, D. (2004). A multilevel test of racial threat theory. *Criminology, 42*(3), 673–698.

Tankebe, J. (2009). Public cooperation with the police in Ghana: Does procedural fairness matter? *Criminology, 47*(4), 1265–1293.

Terrill, W., & Reisig, M. D. (2003). Neighborhood context and police use of force. *Journal of Research in Crime and Delinquency, 40*(3), 291–321.

Thomas, C. W., & Hyman, J. M. (1977). Perceptions of crime, fear of victimization, and public perceptions of police performance. *Journal of Police Science and Administration, 5*, 305–317.

Tyler, T. R., & Wakslak, C. J. (2004). Profiling and police legitimacy: Procedural justice, attributions of motive, and acceptance of police authority. *Criminology, 42*(2), 253–282.

Weitzer, R., & Tuch, S. A. (1999). Race, class, and perceptions of discrimination by the police. *Crime & Delinquency, 45*(4), 494–507.

Wells, W., & Schafer, J. A. (2006). Officer perceptions of police responses to persons with a mental illness. *Policing: An International Journal of Police Strategies & Management, 29*(4), 578–601.

Zamble, E., & Annesley, P. (1987). Some determinants of public attitudes toward the police. *Journal of Police Science and Administration, 15*, 285–290.

COPYRIGHTED MATERIAL — DO NOT DUPLICATE, DISTRIBUTE, OR POST

COPYRIGHTED MATERIAL — DO NOT DUPLICATE, DISTRIBUTE, OR POST

ETHICAL ISSUES AND PROBLEM-SOLVING COURTS

4

SEAN K. WILSON, PhD, AND JASON M. WILLIAMS, PhD

Reading Objectives

- Discuss the definition of problem-solving courts
- Examine the differences between traditional and problem-solving courts
- Discuss the ethical issues associated with problem-solving courts

---

OVERVIEW

Punitive criminal justice policies in the early 1980s have resulted in an expansion of the prison population and an increased processing of nonviolent offenders in courtrooms throughout the United States (Clear & Frost, 2013). To minimize the ever-expanding caseloads that courts face, problem-solving courts have been used as an alternative to the traditional criminal justice system. Problem-solving courts emerged during the 1980s as an attempt to seek justice and lasting change within the judiciary (Wolf, 2008). Traditional courts typically focus on processing cases, while problem-solving courts seek to improve conditions for victims, offenders, and communities impacted by crime and victimization. **Problem-solving courts** take several forms that include drug courts, mental health courts, community courts, and domestic violence courts. There are currently more than 2,500 problem-solving courts throughout the United States (Wolf, 2007). Problem-solving courts are effective in addressing problems that may arise from individuals whose crimes often stem from untreated underlying issues. Rather than simply processing cases and incarcerating defendants in jails and prisons throughout the nation, as traditional courts do, problem-solving courts seek to provide treatment and alternatives to incarceration for participants.

Many of the issues that defendants face in their daily lives are often unaddressed by traditional courts. Thus, problem-solving courts serve as a nontraditional judicial tool to provide therapeutic jurisprudence to defendants, victims, communities, and society as a whole (Wolf, 2007). Several studies have shown that problem-solving courts are effective in reducing recidivism levels, improving the quality of life in communities throughout the United States, and lowering justice-related costs (Brewster, 2001; Peters & Murrin, 2000; Wolfe, Guydish, & Termondt, 2002). In addition, problem-solving courts can also serve as an alternative to incarceration and the adversarial nature of traditional courts by embracing a team-based nonadversarial approach that focuses on interaction among defendants and litigants (Berman, 2004). Moreover, problem-solving courts also seek to involve the community in the justice process by identifying

27

COPYRIGHTED MATERIAL — DO NOT DUPLICATE, DISTRIBUTE, OR POST

COPYRIGHTED MATERIAL — DO NOT DUPLICATE, DISTRIBUTE, OR POST

problems that communities face and creating programs and providing services that seek to engage the community in the justice process. Although there are more than 2,500 problem-solving courts in the United States, the problem-solving movement has not been embraced by all judges, court personnel, and communities, because there are ethical issues that can make the implementation of problem-solving courts throughout the nation difficult (Nored & Carlan, 2008). This chapter will examine the emergence of problem-solving courts (specifically drug courts and community courts) and ethical issues attached to the integration of problem-solving courts.

DRUG COURTS

Traditional courts are often unable to efficiently address social issues that often lead to criminality while attempting to offer solutions to legal problems that emerge in society. Scholars have argued that traditional courts fail to manage the pressing social and cultural needs of populations that are often subject to justice processes, and that problem-solving courts are an alternative way to provide justice to ever-changing environments (Berman, 2004; Birgden, 2004). In the late 1980s crime and incarceration rates increased substantially in the United States (Clear & Frost, 2013). More specifically, drug-related crimes increased, and courts were often overburdened with increasing caseloads. The political atmosphere in the nation at the time called for programs that stressed offender accountability, deterrence, and implementation that was swift (Nored & Carlan, 2008). Because of the public's demand for immediate interventions for offenders, drug courts were seen as a necessary alternative to traditional courts. **Drug courts** are courts that target specific populations of offenders who make up a substantial percentage of the prison population (Lurigio, 2008). These courts seek to merge judicial supervision and mandate treatment for offenders who have drug-abuse problems. Drug courts are different from traditional courts because they attempt to prevent recurring criminal behavior and court involvement by providing social and therapeutic services to defendants. In many ways judges in drug

courts often function as social workers, since they often address psychological and social issues that are not normally addressed by traditional courts.

The first drug court in the United States opened in Miami, Florida, in 1989 (Fulkerson, Keena, & O'Brien, 2012). This court was created to process and provide treatment to nonviolent drug offenders in an attempt to divert repeat drug offenders from recidivating and to end the problem of entering the revolving door of the justice system (Lurigio, 2008). Moreover, the Miami Drug Court allowed participants to voluntarily participate in community drug treatment rather than having their cases processed by traditional courts. Voluntary participation in drug-court treatment programs subjected participants to several conditions, such as agreeing to remain drug free, participating in a court-approved drug-treatment program, submitting to periodic urine analysis, and reporting periodically to the court for supervision (Winick, 2013). If drug-court participants are unable to abide by the guidelines of their drug-treatment program, they will be subjected to a sanction that is agreed on by the participant and the judge (Winick, 2013). If participants are successful in meeting the demands of their drug-treatment program, the judge will dismiss their charges and give them a graduation ceremony, which celebrates their accomplishments in the program in an attempt to approve a drug-court participant's self-worth.

Since the establishment of the Miami Drug Court, states throughout the nation have created drug courts that rely on similar elements of problem-solving courts, which include immediate intervention, a nonadversarial process, intensive judge–offender interaction, an interdisciplinary team approach, and defined rules and goals (Winick, 2013). Currently, there are 2,300 drug courts across the nation (National Drug Court Institute, 2009). Studies have found that drug courts are more effective than traditional courts in reducing recidivism (Fulkerson et al., 2012; Martinez & Eisenberg, 2003). Participants who successfully compete for a drug-court program will often leave the program with no conviction or an expungement of their conviction. Drug courts have two formats, the preadjudication drug court and the postadjudication drug court. In a preadjudication

COPYRIGHTED MATERIAL — DO NOT DUPLICATE. DISTRIBUTE. OR POST

COPYRIGHTED MATERIAL — DO NOT DUPLICATE, DISTRIBUTE, OR POST

drug court, defendants waive their right to a speedy trial, right to a jury trial, and right to confront a witness. If defendants are successful in completing the requirements of the drug-treatment program, their charges are dropped. In the postadjudication drug court, defendants plead guilty to their charges and are placed on probation and transferred to the drug court for supervision (Lurigio, 2008). Both types of drug courts remove participants who are unsuccessful and subject them to the original criminal charges that they faced before admittance to the drug court. Also, drug-court failures face sanctions that are determined by the drug court. Sanctions serve as a deterrent tool for rule violations and the use of illegal substances (Lindquist, Krebs, & Lattimore, 2006).

DRUG-COURT ETHICAL ISSUES

Some courts throughout the nation are wary of implementing the drug-court model because of ethical issues attached to the drug court. For instance, failed drug-court participants may be subject to a harsher sentence than defendants in traditional courts because a participant's inability to abide by the requirements of the drug court can result in the individual having to participate in drug-court programming for a longer period than someone subjected to graduated sanctions in a traditional court (Fulkerson et al., 2012). For example, in a qualitative study of drug-court participants in an Arkansas drug-court program, Fulkerson et al. (2012) found that participants were critical of the drug-court program's lack of confidentiality, one-size-fits-all approach to counseling, judicial subjectivity, and required meeting and employment conflicts. Fulkerson et al. (2012) also note that there are significant disparities between the outcomes for drug-court graduates and noncompliers. Although drug-court participants tend to be satisfied with their drug-court experience, some drug-court participants express concerns.

Participants believe that many drug-court sessions were humiliating and made participants feel self-conscious about their personal issues being shared with other participants in these programs. Also, many participants complained about drug

courts employing counselors who specialize in alcoholism to counsel participants who deal with drug addiction. For drug courts to be effective, personnel must be qualified to address the issues that participants face. Another ethical issue associated with drug courts is that defense attorneys, especially public defenders, believe that working with defendants who are subject to alternative treatments, such as drug courts, falls outside of their responsibilities (Wolf, 2008). Public defenders tend to have an aversion to drug courts because many public defenders are overburdened with underfunded indigent caseloads. Thus, they are often skeptical of drug courts because of their workload and their unwillingness to go beyond traditional lawyering roles and responsibilities to assist their clients.

Judges and prosecutors both object to the social work aspects of problem-solving courts (Berman, 2004). However, judges do tend to support problem-solving courts. For example, 96% of 217 judges who presided over problem-solving courts were very satisfied with their experiences with problem-solving courts (Berman, 2004). Although judges who preside over problem-solving courts tend to support them, many judges do have mixed opinions about problem-solving courts. For instance, a presiding judge of the Seattle Municipal Court who supports problem-solving courts believes that judges should be more concerned with deciding cases and not solving problems (Wolf, 2008). Philosophically speaking, judges tend to favor punishment over rehabilitation as a philosophical preference (Wolf, 2008). Also, judges are often discouraged from participating in problem-solving courts because of their lack of experience in specialized courts. Many judges do not have the necessary training to effectively work in a problem-solving court. Thus, it is imperative that more judges receive the necessary training to prepare them for work within a problem-solving court.

Cost is another factor in regard to whether a judge or prosecutor will be willing to support a drug-court program (Wolf, 2008). Alternative sentences typically cost less than sentencing a defendant to jail or prison time. Thus, judges should be overwhelmingly supportive of alternative sentences such as drug courts. However, the reality is that judges have to deal with overburdened court

COPYRIGHTED MATERIAL — DO NOT DUPLICATE, DISTRIBUTE, OR POST

COPYRIGHTED MATERIAL — DO NOT DUPLICATE, DISTRIBUTE, OR POST

dockets, so they are often skeptical of adding additional burdens to their workload. Judges who are overburdened will often embrace nontraditional alternatives to punishment when such alternatives do not increase or overburden their workload (Wolf, 2008). Prosecutors often object to problem-solving courts because they believe work in such courts is too similar to social work (Wolf, 2008). They often believe that their job is to protect society rather than to fight for the well-being of a client. Thus, their support for drug courts can be mixed. However, many courts throughout the United States have enacted community prosecution programs, which encourage prosecutors to build relationships with communities and stakeholders to respond to crime issues by relying on problem-solving philosophies. Jurisdictions that are concerned with decreasing recidivism may rely on community prosecution. However, community prosecution programs appear to be more concerned with deterring long-term criminality rather than focusing on responding to individual cases and sentences by relying on traditional sentencing philosophies that often ignore the bigger picture goal of solving long-term problems for the benefit of the community.

Although drug courts typically subscribe to a problem-solving jurisprudence that attempts to respond to problems by imposing less harsh sanctions on participants than punitive jurisprudence approaches, problem-solving drug courts often impose sanctions that are just as harsh as traditional courts. Another issue related to drug courts is that many drug courts often target less serious drug offenders (Koetzle, Listwan, Gustaferro, & Kobus, 2015). A meta-analysis of traditional and nontraditional courts by Mitchell, Wilson, Eggers, and MacKenzie (2012) found that 20% of the samples included in their study had minor criminal histories. Also, a study by Schaffer (2006) found that among drug courts reporting participants' criminal history, over half of the courts reported that 50% of drug-court participants had some criminal record. Although drug courts tend to exclude violent offenders from participating in drug courts because they are more likely to recidivate than nonviolent offenders, targeting lower level offenders may have negative consequences for nonviolent offenders. For example, net widening may occur for

nonviolent offenders. Because high-risk offenders often need intensive, community-based supervision, drug courts can serve as a necessary tool to decrease recidivism among violent offenders. A study by Saum and Hiller (2008) that examined post-drug-court data for violent and nonviolent drug-court participants found that participants with a history of violence were no more likely than individuals with no history of violent offending to be rearrested after drug-court participation. Thus, drug courts should closely reconsider excluding violent offenders from drug-court programming, because they can benefit from the resources allocated to such programs.

COMMUNITY COURTS

In the United States the community court movement began when the first such court opened in midtown Manhattan, New York, in 1993 (Sviridoff, Rottman, & Weidner, 2005). Throughout the nation, courts have taken the concepts pioneered by the Manhattan Community Court and have implemented their versions of community courts. **Community courts** seek to repay a community that has been damaged by low-level offending by requiring offenders to repay neighborhoods for their criminality by engaging in community service (Bureau of Justice Assistance, 2000). The community court is similar to traditional courts in that it requires the participation and involvement of police and prosecutors, as well as participation and input from citizens (Boland, 1998). Community courts are created to form partnerships with communities, citizens, and criminal justice practitioners to respond to quality-of-life problems, high crime rates, property disorder, and disorder in an effective manner (Bureau of Justice Assistance, 2000). Traditional courts often embrace a one-size-fits-all approach when responding to crime, without examining or considering input from community members who are most impacted by criminality. Thus, community courts seek to bridge the gap between courts and the communities that they serve.

Citizen advisory boards are responsible for governing each community court and determining

COPYRIGHTED MATERIAL — DO NOT DUPLICATE, DISTRIBUTE, OR POST

COPYRIGHTED MATERIAL — DO NOT DUPLICATE, DISTRIBUTE, OR POST

which crime concerns are the greatest in a given neighborhood and finding solutions to such issues. Community courts often rely on partnerships and resources from city and county agencies and volunteer agencies in the region (Wolf & Worrall, 2004). All community courts rely on a problem-solving and community-focused approach to link offenders to individually based community-based services that seek to provide offenders with job training, drug treatment, and mental health programming when necessary (Lang, 2011). Community courts also rely heavily on improving the accountability of offenders by requiring them to follow community restitution mandates that have consequences for noncompliance. The effectiveness of community courts is determined by collecting and analyzing data and measuring outcomes, cost, and benefits to ensure that community courts are effective in creating systematic change.

The Manhattan Community Court is unique in that it serves the central business district of America's largest cities (Sviridoff et al., 2005). Smaller municipalities throughout the United States have adopted the Manhattan Community Court's model to serve neighborhoods that face various issues. For example, Austin, Texas; Portland, Oregon; Seattle, Washington; Hartford, Connecticut; Brooklyn, New York; Dallas, Texas; Bronx, New York; Santa Ana, California; and other cities throughout the nation have taken innovative approaches to administering justice by creating community-oriented courts (Nugent-Borakove, 2009). The core strengths of community courts are that they respond to adverse social conditions—such as high birth rates among school-age children, low family income, high unemployment rates, low property values, and high crime that many communities experience—by relying on providing social services and resources to individuals impacted by such issues, rather than subjecting such individuals to punishment-oriented policies and responses (Lang, 2011). Relying on community outreach allows court administrators to bridge the gaps between communities and justice agencies. For the most part, empirical data has proved that community courts are effective in reducing recidivism among participants (Nugent-Borakove, 2009; Lee et al., 2013; Henry & Kralstein, 2011). Thus, if community courts are effective in decreasing recidivism and improving the livelihoods of the communities they serve, they should be implemented more frequently.

ETHICAL ISSUES AND COMMUNITY COURTS

Although community courts seek to decrease recidivism, improve the lives of participants, and lower the number of ordinances issued to individuals, in some jurisdictions the numbers of violations have increased (Ammann, 2000). For example, in some jurisdictions, police officers are more inclined to issue more charges for minor offenses (Ammann, 2000). Before community courts, police officers were less likely to issue tickets for minor offenses, because they believed minor charges would be dismissed in court (Ammann, 2000). Thus, sometimes the creation of a community court in a new jurisdiction can result in net widening, since more individuals are likely to be subject to new charges or ordinance violations because police officers are more likely to write tickets if they believe a community court will punish a defendant.

According to Ammann (2000), the homeless specifically are often subject to increased ordinance violations, and their rights are often ignored. Therefore, it is imperative that community court personnel work alongside police agencies to ensure that increased numbers of individuals are not massively being swept into the community court system for minor infractions. Another ethical issue associated with community courts is the reality that some courts handle felonies and family matters. For example, community courts in New York and Minneapolis often handle felonies (Ammann, 2000). The issue associated with community courts handling too large a variety of charges is that individuals who commit minor offenses may be lumped together with violent offenders. Also, community courts often handle cases quickly. Some cases are handled the same day. Handling cases too quickly can infringe on a defendant's right to consult with an attorney or a right to a trial (Ammann, 2000).

Lawyers play an interesting role in the community court system that is different from their role in traditional adversarial courts. For example, lawyers in community courts are expected to shed their

COPYRIGHTED MATERIAL — DO NOT DUPLICATE, DISTRIBUTE, OR POST

COPYRIGHTED MATERIAL — DO NOT DUPLICATE, DISTRIBUTE, OR POST

adversarial role and conform to the goals of the community court (Meekins, 2007). This change in the role may result in defense attorneys having to embrace a culture of underzealous representation. Defense attorneys working in community courts are often overburdened with cases and often unable to effectively investigate cases or seek out alternatives for defendants (Meekins, 2007). Judges in community courts often issue sanctions to defendants to coerce compliance with treatment or conditions issued by a court. Usually, when a defendant agrees to sanctions, such sanctions are automatic and non-negotiable (Meekins, 2007).

However, in jurisdictions where challenges are accepted, defense attorneys are often discouraged and sometimes met with anger from judges. Thus, many defense attorneys are less likely to challenge sanctions, even when a defendant wants to challenge a sanction, which is a violation of the attorney's ethical rules. Because the roles of attorneys, judges, and case managers are different in nonadversarial community courts than adversarial courts, defendants are discouraged from challenging recommended treatment, denied their right to remain silent, and denied other constitutional guarantees (Meekins, 2007). Also, attorney–client confidentiality may be breached by the interaction with third parties.

Judges working in community courts play a major role in administering justice, which allows them the ability to schedule hearings with defendants that may take place without an attorney present (Meekins, 2007). Because judges often address defendants directly and intensely, defendants can be pressured into making incriminating statements. Also, defendants may be coerced to accept treatments that may not be beneficial for the defendant. Because judges' role in a community court differs from their role in a traditional court, it is imperative that judges are individuals who truly care about the well-being of their clients. Judges who are punishment oriented are not a good fit for community courts. The role of defense attorneys in community courts must be examined to determine if their often minimized role in the community court setting violates ethical standards.

CONCLUSION

Problem-solving courts are effective in addressing crimes that may be related to issues in society. Their less punitive approach to administering justice grants defendants the ability to receive treatment and make amends for their criminality by allowing defendants the ability to provide services to their community. Problem-solving courts are effective in reducing recidivism, and they serve as a nonpunitive alternative to tough-on-crime criminal justice policies. Problem-solving courts are effective in addressing underlying issues that are often ignored by traditional courts because of increased docket loads. Problem-solving courts seek to provide individualized justice to individuals who often need individualized treatment. Although there are many ethical issues associated with problem-solving courts, such issues can be remedied by providing effective training to problem-solving court personnel. Overall, problem-solving courts provide a much-needed alternative to punishment in a time when alternatives to incarceration are being embraced by scholars, policy makers, and society.

Discussion Questions

1   What is a problem-solving court?
2   What are the differences between traditional and problem-solving courts?
3   What is a drug court?
4   What is a community court?
5   What are some ethical issues associated with drug and community courts?

COPYRIGHTED MATERIAL — DO NOT DUPLICATE, DISTRIBUTE, OR POST

COPYRIGHTED MATERIAL — DO NOT DUPLICATE, DISTRIBUTE, OR POST

REFERENCES

Ammann, J. J. (2000). Addressing quality of life crimes in our cities: Criminalization, community courts and community compassion. *Saint Louis University Law Journal, 44*, 811–820.

Berman, G. (2004). Redefining criminal courts: Problem solving and the meaning of justice. *American Criminal Law Review, 41*, 1313–1319.

Birgden, A. (2004). Therapeutic jurisprudence and good lives: A rehabilitation framework for corrections. *Psychology, Crime & Law, 10*, 180–186.

Boland, B. (1998). Community prosecution: Portland's experience. In D. R. Karp (Ed.), *Community justice: An emerging field* (pp. 253–255). Lanham, MD: Rowman & Littlefield.

Brewster, M. P. (2001). An evaluation of the Chester County (PA) drug court program. *Journal of Drug Issues, 31*, 177–206.

Bureau of Justice Assistance. (2000). *Community courts: An evolving model*. Washington, DC: US Department of Justice Office of Justice Programs.

Clear, T. R., & Frost, N. A. (2013). *The punishment imperative: The rise and failure of mass incarceration in America*. New York: NYU Press.

Fulkerson, A., Keena, L. D., & O'Brien, E. (2012). Understanding success and nonsuccess in the drug court. *International Journal of Offender Therapy and Comparative Criminology, 57*(10), 1297–1316.

Henry, K., & Kralstein, D. (2011). *Community courts: The research literature*. Washington, DC: Bureau of Justice Statistics.

Koetzle, D., Listwan, S., Gustaferro, W., & Kobus, K. (2015). Treating high-risk offenders in the community: The potential of drug courts. *International Journal of Offender Therapy and Comparative Criminology, 59*(5), 449–465.

Lang, J. (2011). *What is a community court?* Washington, DC: Bureau of Justice Assistance.

Lee, C. G., Rottman, D., Swaner, R., Lambson, S., Rempel, M., & Curtis, R. (2013). *A community court grows in Brooklyn: A comprehensive evaluation of the Red Hook Community Justice Center*. Williamsburg, VA: National Center for State Courts.

Lindquist, C. H., Krebs, C. P., & Lattimore, P. K. (2006). Sanctions and rewards in drug court programs: Implementation, perceived efficacy, and decision making. *Journal of Drug Issues, 36*(1), 119–146.

Lurigio, A. (2008). First 20 years of drug treatment courts: A brief description of their history and impact. *Federal Probation: A Journal of Correctional Philosophy and Practice, 72*, 13–17.

Martinez, A. I., & Eisenberg, M. (2003). *Initial process and outcome evaluation of drug courts in Texas*. Austin: Texas Criminal Justice Policy Council.

Meekins, T. M. (2007). Risky business: Criminal specialty courts and the ethical obligations of the zealous criminal defender. *Berkeley Journal of Criminal Law, 12*(75), 75–126.

Mitchell, O., Wilson, D., Eggers, A., & MacKenzie, D. (2012). Assessing the effectiveness of drug courts on recidivism: A meta-analytic review of traditional and non-traditional drug courts. *Journal of Criminal Justice, 40*, 60–71.

National Drug Court Institute. (2009). *Drug court review*. Alexandria, VA: Author.

Nored, L. S., & Carlan, P. E. (2008). Success of drug court programs: Examination of the perceptions of drug court personnel. *Criminal Justice Review, 33*(3), 329–342.

Nugent-Borakove, M. E. (2009). *Seattle Municipal Community Court: Outcome evaluation final report*. Arlington, VA: Justice Management Institute.

Peters, R., & Murrin, M. R. (2000). Effectiveness of treatment-based drug courts in reducing criminal recidivism. *Criminal Justice and Behavior, 1*, 72–96.

Saum, C. A., & Hiller, M. (2008). Should violent offenders be excluded from drug court participation? An examination of the recidivism of violent and nonviolent drug court participants. *Criminal Justice Review, 33*(3), 291–307.

Schaffer, D. K. (2006). *Reconsidering drug court effectiveness: A meta-analytic review* (Doctoral dissertation, University of Cincinnati).

Sviridoff, M., Rottman, D. B., & Weidner, R. (2005). *Dispensing justice locally*. New York: Center for Court Innovation.

Winick, B. J. (2013). Problem solving courts: Therapeutic jurisprudence in practice. In R. L. Weiner and E. M. Brank (Eds.), *Problem solving courts* (pp. 211–236). New York: Springer.

Wolf, R. V. (2007). *Principles of problem-solving justice*. New York: Center for Court Innovation.

Wolf, R. V. (2008). Breaking with tradition: Introducing problem solving in conventional courts. *International Review of Law, Computers & Technology, 22*, 77–93.

Wolf, R. V., & Worrall, J. L. (2004). *Lessons from the field: Ten community prosecution leadership profiles*. Alexandria, VA: American Prosecutors Research Institute.

Wolfe, E., Guydish, J., & Termondt, J. (2002). A drug court outcome evaluation comparing arrests in a two year follow-up period. *Journal of Drug Issues, 32*, 1155–1171.

COPYRIGHTED MATERIAL — DO NOT DUPLICATE, DISTRIBUTE, OR POST

COPYRIGHTED MATERIAL — DO NOT DUPLICATE, DISTRIBUTE, OR POST

COPYRIGHTED MATERIAL — DO NOT DUPLICATE. DISTRIBUTE. OR POST

COPYRIGHTED MATERIAL — DO NOT DUPLICATE, DISTRIBUTE, OR POST

5 | THE PRISON INDUSTRIAL COMPLEX

VIVIAN C. SMITH, PhD

Reading Objectives

- Define the prison industrial complex
- Describe how the privatization of prisons, jails, and detention centers feeds into the prison industrial complex
- Examine and explain the main controversial issues surrounding the prison industrial complex

---

OVERVIEW

Early forms of punishment in America were carried over from England. However, due to major changes in American history, the purpose and methods used for punishment have changed numerous times. Nevertheless, prisons became institutions built primarily for the purpose of depriving convicted individuals of their freedom and thus keeping them from the general public.

Early in America, punishment for crimes was mostly based on a **retributive philosophy**. This form of justice implies that offenders should be punished equivalently to the crime committed (Murphy, 1973). The retributive philosophy was evident by the forms of punishment utilized; for example, the ducking stool, the gag, stocks, pillories, whipping, capital punishment, and so forth. The development of prisons came later, during the 1700s, with the construction of a double-purpose prison that served as a copper mine and also housed prisoners of war from the American Revolution. Prisoners lived underground and were submitted

to hard labor. The Old Newgate Prison, located in Connecticut, was the first official U.S. prison and came much earlier than the often-mentioned Walnut Street Jail established in 1790 (Hanser, 2013). According to Hanser (2013), the accurate chronological history of American penology is significant, since it shows "the development of prison construction and correctional thought, which occurred over the span of years with many lessons that were hard-learned" (p. 26).

Nevertheless, during the Age of Enlightenment, several philosophers questioned the purpose of punishment and were often seen as advocates for humane treatment of prisoners. Philosophers such as William Penn (1644–1718), Charles de Montesquieu (1689–1755), Voltaire (1694–1778), Cesare Beccaria (1738–1794), John Howard (1726–1790), and Jeremy Bentham (1748–1832) challenged traditional (often religion-based) ideas of torture, criminal responsibility, justice, punishment, and corrections. Nevertheless, in the 1970s Michel Foucault (1975) further disputed the idea that prisons and jails were a more humanitarian form of punishment than their earlier

COPYRIGHTED MATERIAL — DO NOT DUPLICATE, DISTRIBUTE, OR POST

COPYRIGHTED MATERIAL — DO NOT DUPLICATE, DISTRIBUTE, OR POST

"corporal punishment" predecessors. Doty and Wheatley (2013) argue that Foucault's analysis of punishment provides insight into the prison industrial complex (PIC). Foucault (1975) examines the confinement of persons (in prison, jails, etc.) as a function of social control. The imprisonment of persons during the current era of mass incarceration (supported by research and government statistics) seems to be targeted to a specific segment of the population: the poor, the marginalized, and people of color (Alexander, 2012; Doty & Wheatley, 2013). Another argument connected to the PIC, from Foucault's writing (1975), was the differentiation between the powerful and persons economically deprived (Doty & Wheatley, 2013). Thus, those who argue that the PIC exists find its roots in the United States' (and several other countries') initial purpose of punishment, and perhaps the lack of clarity for the true purpose of prisons, jails, and detention centers. Some argued that punishment does not deter others from committing crime and in fact increases recidivism (Foucault, 1975; Wehr & Aseltine, 2013). Lastly, the expansion of the PIC could be simply reduced to a country's system of capitalism, in which several "industries" are controlled by private owners for profit, rather than by the state.

DEFINITION

One of the consistent aspects of the definition of the PIC is the profit gained by various parties from the criminalization of "deviant behavior" and the incarceration of people, provided they violate the norm. In addition to the profitability of punishment, there are key players involved within the "complex." These include, but are not limited to, government officials, corporations, and most importantly, the prisoners themselves. It is important to highlight the variability in definitions of the PIC. This variability demonstrates the dissent, or perhaps individual ideological frameworks, by which several researchers choose to explore the macro and micro systems that fuel the PIC.

Below are several definitions of the PIC that incorporate varying features:

Definition 1: "a profiteering system fueled by the economic interest of private corporations, federal and state correctional institutions and politicians." (Fulcher, 2012, p. 589)

Definition 2: "The prison-industrial complex is an interweaving of private business and government interests, extremely profitable." (Evans, 2005, p. 216)

Definition 3: "PIC as an economic system involves both the State and private corporations working in collaboration to profit imprisonment: The State secures employment for communities where prisons are held; private corporations profit from the construction and maintenance of prisons; and both profit from extracted prison labor." (Raza, 2011, p. 167)

Definition 4: "a set of governmental, private and corporate interests that develop policies and practices in order to exert social, political and economic control, and to perpetuate social processes that are biased by race, class, gender and political perspective." (Wehr & Aseltine, 2013, p. 2)

For purposes of this text, the **prison industrial complex** is defined as a system that utilizes lobbying strategies from private entities and corporations to encourage government agencies and politicians to incarcerate persons (disproportionately women, people of color, and the poor) for profit, which is then to be distributed among powerful stakeholders. The discussion surrounding the PIC includes a variety of notorious issues within our society. Many of these issues often surface when referring to mass imprisonment in the United States. America currently imprisons over 1.5 million people and has one of the largest prison systems in the world (Carson & Golinelli, 2014; Pratt, 2009; Sentencing Project, 2015). The ostentatious title of being the number one "incarcerator" in the world is not without controversy.

COPYRIGHTED MATERIAL — DO NOT DUPLICATE, DISTRIBUTE, OR POST

COPYRIGHTED MATERIAL — DO NOT DUPLICATE, DISTRIBUTE, OR POST

CONTROVERSIAL ISSUES

HISTORY

The philosophy behind the PIC parallels that of a southern system of penology, where concepts such as convict leasing, chain gangs, and prison farm labor impacted the way formal punishment was carried out by corrections officials. All of these concepts are linked through a common thread and are often a controversial topic in America: race. One of the main existing contentions is that the criminal justice system—more specifically, the current corrections system—is a racialized form of social control, just as Jim Crow was in the late 1800s and up through the Civil Rights Act (Alexander, 2012), and that this system is fueled by the PIC.

Prison labor was a feature of prison development in the United States. It is mainly associated with the **Auburn prison system**, a penal method in which inmates were kept in solitary confinement during the night and were supposed to work during the day ("Auburn System," 2015), often to offset the costs of their stay. However, it was not until the post–Civil War era that a more formalized system was established to make prisons economically self-sufficient and profitable. This is known as the **convict lease system**. Under this system, prisoners worked labor-intensive jobs under private contractors/companies within prison workshops and were mandated to do so through the state (Raza, 2011). Inmate labor would then become more lucrative for the state and private contractors. Industries that signed lease agreements during this time would pay a fee to house, feed, clothe, and guard inmates (Raza, 2011; Thompson, 2012). Thus, much like the PIC, convict leasing provided a way for private companies and the state to maximize profit from cheap labor by minimizing costs (i.e., substandard shelter, food, clothing, and unqualified guards).

Additional features of southern penology that profited from inmate labor were chain gangs and prison farms. Chain gang labor (early 1900s) was mostly used to build the infrastructure within the state (e.g., roads, railroads, state highways). Inmates were shackled at all times, slept in cages, and endured arduous weather. As was customary at the time, "rebellious" prisoners often suffered extreme discipline practices such as whippings from brute, unskilled guards. As states began to abolish convict lease systems, prison farms began to sprout in the late 1930s. These were very similar to prior slave plantations in the South. The purpose, as with the convict lease system, was prison self-sustainability. Nonetheless, inmates suffered some of the same grueling issues associated with earlier forms of convict leasing. However, decline in profitability made this type of system less desirable and it was eventually dismantled (Roth, 2006).

Prior to the Civil War, particularly in the South, enslaved African Americans were not imprisoned at the same rate as Whites. In fact, most prisons were filled with Whites because detaining Blacks would conflict with and prevent plantation owners from fully profiting from slavery. However, after the Civil War, 90% of the prison population became African American. According to Gabbidon (2012), W. E. B. Du Bois interpreted the transformation of the prison population in the United States as a direct result of the emancipation of African Americans. According to Raza (2011), post-emancipation Black codes legislation became a way to regain control of freed slaves. Black codes delineated and prohibited socially deviant behavior in the United States in terms of race (Davis, 2003). Vagrancy laws, labor contract laws, and travel restrictions were the catalyst that turned newly freed slaves into prisoners and thus subject, again, to involuntary servitude through the formation of the convict lease system. As Du Bois described it, "a new slavery and slave-trade was established" (as cited in Gabbidon, 2012, p. 62). Brewer and Heitzeg (2008) argue that similar to the institution of the convict leasing system, the PIC is able to thrive as a color-blind racist regime because crime and punishment elude issues of race by setting a discourse based on the eradication of social evils such as drugs, gangs, and crime.

PRIVATIZATION OF PUNISHMENT

Although the PIC has been deemed as some sort of conspiracy theory and dismissed by some lawmakers, evidence shows that the profitability gathered from incarceration is not mythical. At the center

COPYRIGHTED MATERIAL — DO NOT DUPLICATE. DISTRIBUTE. OR POST

COPYRIGHTED MATERIAL — DO NOT DUPLICATE, DISTRIBUTE, OR POST

of the PIC is the corporate influence of two major private prison companies: the Corrections Corporation of America (CCA) and the GEO Group (Bowie, 2012; Doty & Wheatley, 2013; Evans, 2005; Fulcher, 2012; Thompson, 2012). Together, the two companies exert control over more than 100 facilities in the United States (CCA, 2015; GEO Group, 2015). These companies have state, federal, and local contracts to manage or operate prisons, jails, detention centers, and residential halfway houses across the United States. Besides local and state governments, they also own contracts with the U.S. Marshals Service, U.S. Immigration and Customs Enforcement (ICE), and the Federal Bureau of Prisons (BOP; Bowie, 2012; Doty & Wheatley, 2013).

The CCA was first established in 1983 by Tom Beasley, the former chair of the Tennessee Republican Party (Bowie, 2012; Culp, 2011). The CCA opened its first privatized facilities in Houston, Texas, in 1984. Its first customer was the Immigration and Naturalization Service; the facilities held illegal immigrants awaiting deportation (Doty & Wheatley, 2013; Wood, 2007). The GEO Group is the second largest private prison company, formerly known as the Wackenhut Corrections Corporation. The company also began to operate private detention facilities in 1984 (Doty & Wheatley, 2013; Wood, 2007). As other private prison companies were created, the revenues of such businesses surpassed the billion-dollar mark, and Wall Street began to offer bonds and securities from prison companies to individual investors and mutual funds (Wood, 2007). In April 2015 Columbia University became the first institution of higher education in America to dissociate itself from private prison profits (Chan, 2015). This meant that the university would sell thousands of the shares it holds of two of the biggest private prison companies, including the CCA (Chan, 2015). The decision came after a student-based campaign drew attention to the investment in private prisons as incentivized by higher convictions, longer sentences, and benefiting from a racially disparate system (Chan, 2015).

Additional companies have also benefited from the PIC by minimizing their operation costs through the cheap labor of prisoners. Companies that use prison labor include IMB, Motorola, Honeywell, Microsoft, Boeing, Starbucks, Victoria's Secret, and Revlon (Bowie, 2012; Evans, 2005; Thompson, 2012). Inmates are often paid $0.12 to $1.15 per hour; a fraction of what these industries would have to pay in wages on the outside and even in alternative workforces in Mexico or Southeast Asia (Thompson, 2012). Several other companies benefit from prison construction and the privatization of prisons because this offers additional sectors or consumers for their services (e.g., AT&T, Sprint, Western Union, and Aramark; Raza, 2011).

Private prison companies run on a business model. That is, the main purpose is turning a profit. The state and federal governments pay private companies per inmate, per day, so profits depend on the minimum expenditure amount to operate daily (Bowie, 2012; Evans, 2005; Raza, 2011). As a result of cutting costs, human violations have been reported; these include substandard diets, inadequate health care, dangerous workplaces, and poorly trained staff (Evans, 2005; Thompson, 2012). Increasing profitability by decreasing expenditure (at any cost, including health and safety) is a main component of the PIC. This is ubiquitous to imprisonment and not unique to the private corporations mentioned above. The federal government also profits from this model of capitalism. UNICOR is a government corporation within the BOP, created by Congress in 1934 that provides employment to staff and inmates at federal prisons throughout the United States. UNICOR sells a variety of consumer products and services, such as office furniture, clothing and textiles, electronics, and industrial products such as security fencing, vehicle tags, and recycling services (Office of the Inspector General, 2010). A report by the Office of the Inspector General (2010) calculated that UNICOR employed "approximately 19,000 inmates and generated total revenues of approximately $1 billion" (p. 10). The same report pointed to an investigation of e-waste from UNICOR's recycling business after several complaints by inmates and staff. The results of the investigation pointed to numerous failures by UNICOR that violated health, safety, and environmental laws. Failure to abide by these regulations unnecessarily exposed inmates, BOP staff, and UNICOR staff to high, toxic levels of cadmium and lead while working in recycling activities. Lastly, the Office of the Inspector General also found that prior

COPYRIGHTED MATERIAL — DO NOT DUPLICATE, DISTRIBUTE, OR POST

COPYRIGHTED MATERIAL — DO NOT DUPLICATE, DISTRIBUTE, OR POST

to 2009, "UNICOR failed to promptly act on the requests of Safety Managers when the requests conflicted with UNICOR's business priorities" (p. xii).

THE WAR ON DRUGS AND THE PIC

On the forefront of the PIC is the steady increase in the number of people sentenced to prison. According to several studies, the numerous laws making up what we call today "the war on drugs" legislation has been one of the main factors for the increase in thousands of persons sentenced to prison (Alexander, 2012; Bush-Baskette & Smith, 2012; Mauer & King, 2007; Travis, Western, & Redburn, 2014; Pratt, 2009). In 1972 President Richard Nixon announced the commencement of what would become the "war on drugs." This was in response to the public's panic over the rise of drug use among young people. However, it was not until the Ronald Reagan and George H. W. Bush administrations that a greater emphasis was put on tough law enforcement (Walker, 2001). Therefore, it is not surprising that the dominant reason for the population growth in U.S. prisons since 1980 is drug offending (Mumola & Karberg, 2006; Blumstein & Beck, 1999).

The rapid growth was even more significant for women and minorities (Blumstein & Beck, 1999; Steffensmeier & Demuth, 2000). It has been argued that such increase is due to punitive criminal justice policies that underlie the war on drugs. These include increase in arrests, drug law enforcement, and sentencing changes. Evidence of racial and gender drug-sentencing disparities began to emerge in the latter 1960s with the creation of the most draconian drug laws ever established: the New York Rockefeller Drug Laws (RDL). The sentencing mechanism of the RDL became a platform for mandatory sentencing laws throughout the United States. Under these laws, an A-1 felony (possession of 2 ounces or sale of 1 ounce of an illegal narcotic) required a mandatory sentence of 15 to 25 years or life (Tinto, 2001). Prior to the conception of the RDL, a person needed 16 ounces to acquire the same sentence. These laws, like most mandatory minimum sentencing laws, removed all the discretion from the judges. **Mandatory minimum** sentences require that a judge impose a minimum length of

incarceration regardless of any other factors or mitigating circumstances (these sentences require that individuals serve longer prison terms). This type of sentencing is part of a determinate sentencing system. **Determinate sentencing** consists of fixed periods of incarceration with no flexibility in the amount of time served (Hanser, 2013). Although the implementation of determinate sentencing was supposed to add uniformity to sentencing by way of reducing judges' discretion, empirical studies have contradicted this thesis and in fact found further inconsistencies in sentencing, particularly for people of color (Cano & Spohn, 2012; Lyons, Lurigio, Roque, & Rodriguez, 2013; Spohn & Sample, 2013).

In the 1980s the war on drugs focused on the arrest of low-level drug dealers for possession and/or trafficking of "controlled dangerous substances." In particular, the drug policies contained in the Anti-Drug Abuse Acts of 1986 and 1988 dramatically increase the number of women and people of color in state and federal prisons (Bush-Baskette, 2010; Bush-Baskette & Smith, 2012). Mandatory sentencing schemes, along with the disparity in sentencing of crack versus powder cocaine, were catalysts that subjected individuals to a greater probability of longer periods of incarceration in state and federal prison systems (Travis, Western, & Redburn, 2014). For approximately 3 decades, a person would need 100 grams of powder cocaine to obtain the same sentence as a person with only 1 gram of crack (often denoted as the 100:1 disparity). In 2010 Congress passed the Fair Sentencing Act, which decreased the sentencing ratio from 100:1 to 18:1. Several advocacy groups hoped that in later years, the sentencing disparity would be eliminated entirely.

Overall, the laws explained above were catalysts for the development and preservation of the PIC. Fulcher (2012) posited that as the prison population grew, due mainly to war on drugs, tolerance for higher taxes in order to pay for inmates diminished, thus allowing government officials to seek alternative options from private agencies to "solve" the prison boom crisis. In an attempt to solve the overcrowding in prisons due to tough crime legislation, government officials turned to a for-profit system to manage mass imprisonment in America (Wood, 2007).

COPYRIGHTED MATERIAL — DO NOT DUPLICATE, DISTRIBUTE, OR POST

COPYRIGHTED MATERIAL — DO NOT DUPLICATE, DISTRIBUTE, OR POST

"CRIMMIGRATION"

Researchers, policy makers and advocates have also shed light on an issue that is closely aligned with the PIC. The immigration industrial complex has also been recognized as part of a for-profit system involving government policies, immigrant detention, and the privatization of immigration centers (Douglas & Sáenz, 2013; Doty & Wheatley, 2013; Garcia-Hernández, 2014). Closely aligned with this section of the "complex" is crimmigration. The term **crimmigration** signifies the intersection of criminal law and immigration legislation (Garcia-Hernández, 2014); that is, the use of criminal justice practices to manage illegal immigrants in the United States, in particular those of Hispanic descent. This practice became widely used in 2005 when the U.S. Department of Justice and the U.S. Department of Homeland Security launched Operation Streamline, which required all migrants crossing the border illegally to now be charged with a misdemeanor or felony and be returned to their home country. This act was previously handled through a civil (not criminal) immigration system. According to a report by the U.S. Department of Homeland Security (Office of the Inspector General, 2015), the effectiveness of such an initiative is unknown, due to the U.S. Border Patrol's inability to measure its effect based on the initial goals: to increase overall removals, decrease illegal reentry, and decrease general costs. In fact, the report highlights that the only certain outcome was that the switch to a criminal system has increased the workload of southwestern Border Patrol officers.

The use of crimmigration has led to an even larger privatization of the corrections movement in the United States, which is mainly characterized by the detention of illegal immigrants awaiting criminal charges and/or deportation (Douglas & Sáenz, 2013; Stumpf, 2011). The anti-immigration rhetoric that exists in the United States has been one of the driving sources for the expansion of the immigration industrial complex. The benefactors of such rhetoric, as with the larger complex, are corporations like the CCA and GEO Group. The ICE holds approximately 17% of its detainees in contracted detention facilities, and 13% are held in ICE-owned facilities but are often managed by private corporations like the CCA and GEO Group (Doty & Wheatley, 2013). These powerhouse groups have used their power to influence policy decisions regarding immigration reform, such as Arizona's controversial anti–illegal immigration bill, otherwise known as Arizona's Support Our Law Enforcement and Safe Neighborhoods Act, or Senate Bill 1070, in 2010 (Doty & Wheatley, 2013): a controversial and highly debated piece of legislation, which required law enforcement officers to determine an individual's immigration status during a lawful/routine stop if the officer suspected illegal residential status. Critics of the law, such as the American Civil Liberties Union (ACLU), suggested that this could induce further racial/ethnic profiling in America.

Nevertheless, the passage and the later consent of S.B. 1070 by the U.S. Supreme Court (*Arizona v. United States*, 2012) was a key success to those who directly benefit from prison privatization. In fact, a journalistic investigation discovered that former Arizona governor Jan Brewer's spokesperson and her campaign manager were both former lobbyists for the major private prison companies (Kirkham, 2012). But the CCA and GEO Group have profited from local and federal governmental policy decisions before. The passage of the 1996 Illegal Immigration Reform and Immigrant Responsibility Act, which permitted "an increased demand for detention beds," allowed the CCA and GEO Group to be awarded several government contracts.

Privatization of immigration detention centers has exposed increased human and constitutional violations to detainees. According to a 2012 report by the ACLU, which investigated and toured several immigration facilities in Georgia—including the largest for-profit detention center—there are clear inadequacies in the living conditions and physical and mental health care of the detainees. In addition, there have been reports of massive abuses of power by those in charge in private detention centers in several states (ACLU, 2011, 2012). The most recent report also makes several recommendations to the government that would curtail the "handling" of immigrants as products through a for-profit immigration system.

COPYRIGHTED MATERIAL — DO NOT DUPLICATE, DISTRIBUTE, OR POST

COPYRIGHTED MATERIAL — DO NOT DUPLICATE, DISTRIBUTE, OR POST

CASE STUDY: "KIDS FOR CASH"

Perhaps the most noticeable case of the PIC was illustrated in Luzerne County in northeastern Pennsylvania. In February 2009 two judges, Mark A. Ciavarella and Michael T. Conahan, pleaded guilty to tax evasion and wire fraud after a federal investigation linked the two to a scheme in which the judges gained approximately $2.6 million in kickbacks for sentencing and sending juveniles to two private detention centers (Frank, 2009; Urbina, 2009). Ciavarella ran the juvenile court for 12 years, and Conahan was on the county's Court of Common Pleas (Urbina, 2009).

The plan included a wealthy injury lawyer who wanted to build a private detention center. The friends co-opted a scheme not only to build but also to supply "bodies" into the new private juvenile detention facilities, PA Child Care and Western PA Child Care. The power of these two judges allowed the public, state-run, facility to be defunded permanently so that the only locations and detention centers available would be the new private detention centers owned by their friend. Ciavarella in particular increased the number of juveniles in these private facilities by apparently upholding a zero-tolerance courtroom (Frank, 2009; Urbina, 2009). In 2006 a 13-year-old was sent to one of the juvenile detention centers for failing to appear in court to serve as a witness to a fight at school. The parents claimed they were never notified about the hearing (Urbina, 2009). The plot unraveled after federal investigators were tipped off by state auditors, who noticed discrepancies in the number and amount being billed to the state for each juvenile and the centers' inability to pay their utility bills (for more, see the *Kids for Cash* documentary).

CONCLUSION

Several scholars have argued that the PIC is mainly fueled by a for-profit business model sustained by laws that criminalize behavior and increase penalties/sentences. Whether the complex is intentional or not varies in opinion by those who play a part in it or are affected by it. Nevertheless, what is clear is that the PIC represents the intersection of the racialization of crime, political capital, and capitalism. Acknowledging the controversial issues surrounding the PIC, particularly at higher levels of government, could potentially lead to informed political decisions and further criminal justice policies that could affect the future rate of imprisonment.

Finally, it is important not to confound the PIC with prison labor to offset the costs of imprisonment. The inclusion of private companies and investors complicates the discourse surrounding the use of prisoners, as bodies or workers, to enhance a private economy. In fact, some have argued that the economic impact of cheap labor by prisoners is detrimental to the overall American economy (Thompson, 2012). Those lobbying for harsher sentences for nonviolent offenses on behalf of companies such as the CCA and GEO Group are not particularly concerned with the safety of citizens; instead, they are interested in the entry-level (low-priced) labor that an influx of additional inmates would contribute to their companies. Lastly, claims that the construction of prisons enhances the economic trends in towns where they are built have been challenged. A research study found no significant difference between seven rural counties in New York that hosted a prison versus another seven counties that did not (King, Mauer, & Huling, 2003).

Discussion Questions

1 Does the lack of a universal definition of the PIC diminish its existence?

2 What ethical issues arise based on the PIC?

3 How is the convict lease system similar to the PIC?

4 Based on the controversial issues, should laws be in place to curtail the individual profiting of sentencing persons to prisons/detention centers? Why or why not?

5 Due to the country's state of mass incarceration, is the PIC necessary for the sustainability of prisons?

COPYRIGHTED MATERIAL — DO NOT DUPLICATE, DISTRIBUTE, OR POST

COPYRIGHTED MATERIAL — DO NOT DUPLICATE, DISTRIBUTE, OR POST

REFERENCES

Alexander, M. (2012). *The new Jim Crow: Mass incarceration in the age of colorblindness*. New York, NY: New Press.

American Civil Liberties Union of Arizona. (2011). *In their own words*. Phoenix, AZ: Author. Retrieved from http://www.acluaz.org/sites/default/files/documents/detention%20report%202011.pdf

American Civil Liberties Union of Georgia. (2012). Prisoners of profit: Immigrant and detention in Georgia. Atlanta, GA: Author. Retrieved from http://www.acluga.org/files/2713/3788/2900/Prisoners_of_Profit.pdf

Auburn system. (2015). In *Encyclopedia Britannica*. Retrieved from http://www.britannica.com/topic/Auburn-system

Blumstein, A., & Beck, A. J. (1999). Population growth in U.S. prisons, 1980–1996. In M. Tonry & J. Petersilia (Eds.), *Crime and justice* (pp.17–61). Chicago, IL: University of Chicago Press.

Bowie, N. (2012). Profit driven prison industrial complex: The economics of incarceration in the USA. *Centre for Research on Globalization*, 6.

Brewer, R. M., & Heitzeg, N. A. (2008). The racialization of crime and punishment, criminal justice, color-blind racism, and the political economy of the prison industrial complex. *American Behavioral Scientist, 51*(5), 625–644.

Bush-Baskette, S. R. (2010). *Misguided justice: The war on drugs and the incarceration of Black women*. Bloomington, IN: iUniverse.

Bush-Baskette, S. R., & Smith, V. C. (2012). Is meth the new crack for women in the war on drugs? Factors affecting sentencing outcomes for women and parallels between meth and crack. *Feminist Criminology, 7*(1), 48–69.

Cano, M. V., & Spohn, C. (2012). Circumventing the penalty for offenders facing mandatory minimums revisiting the dynamics of "sympathetic" and "salvageable" offenders. *Criminal Justice and Behavior, 39*(3), 308–332.

Carson, E. A., & Golinelli, D. (2014). *Prisoners in 2013*. Washington, DC: Bureau of Justice Statistics.

Chan, W. (2015). Columbia becomes first U.S. university to divest from prisons. Retrieved from http://www.cnn.com/2015/06/23/us/columbia-university-prison-divest

Corrections Corporation of America. (2015). Locations. Retrieved from http://www.cca.com/locations

Culp, R. (2011). The failed promise of prison privatization. *Prison Legal News, 22*(10). Retrieved from https://www.prisonlegalnews.org/news/2011/oct/15/the-failed-promise-of-prison-privatization

Davis, A. (2003). *Are prisons obsolete?* New York, NY: Seven Stories Press.

Doty, R. L., & Wheatley, E. S. (2013). Private detention and the immigration industrial complex. *International Political Sociology, 7*(4), 426–443.

Douglas, K. M., & Sáenz, R. (2013). The criminalization of immigrants & the immigration-industrial complex. *Daedalus, 142*(3), 199–227.

Evans, L. (2005). Playing global cop: US militarism and the prison industrial complex. In J. Sudbury, ed., *Global lockdown: Race, gender, and the prison–industrial complex* (215–227). London: Routledge.

Foucault, M. (1975). *Discipline and punishment*. London: Allen Lane.

Frank, T. (2009, April 1). Thomas Frank says "kids for cash" incentivizes the prison industry. *Wall Street Journal*. Retrieved from http://www.wsj.com/articles/SB123854010220075533

Fulcher, P. A. (2012). Hustle and flow: Prison privatization fueling the prison industrial complex. *Washburn Law Journal, 51*(3).

Gabbidon, M. S. L. (2012). *W. E. B. Du Bois on crime and justice: Laying the foundations of sociological criminology*. Abingdon, UK: Routledge.

García-Hernández, C. C. (2014). Creating crimmigration. *Brigham Young University Law Review, 2013*(6), 1457–1516.

GEO Group. (2015). Locations. Retrieved from http://www.geogroup.com/locations

Hanser, R. D. (2013). *Introduction to corrections*. Thousand Oaks, CA: Sage.

King, R. S., Mauer, M., & Huling, T. (2003). *Big prisons, small towns: Prison economics in rural America*. Washington, DC: Sentencing Project.

Kirkham, C. (2012, June 7). Private prisons profit from immigration crackdown, federal and local law enforcement partnerships. *Huffington Post*. Retrieved from http://www.huffingtonpost.com/2012/06/07/private-prisons-immigration-federal-lawenforcement_n_1569219.html

Lyons, T., Lurigio, A. J., Roque, L., & Rodriguez, P. (2013). Racial disproportionality in the criminal justice system for drug offenses: A state legislative response to the problem. *Race and Justice, 3*(1), 83–101.

Mauer, M., & King, R. S. (2007). Uneven justice: State rates of incarceration by race and ethnicity. Washington, DC: Sentencing Project.

COPYRIGHTED MATERIAL — DO NOT DUPLICATE, DISTRIBUTE, OR POST

COPYRIGHTED MATERIAL — DO NOT DUPLICATE, DISTRIBUTE, OR POST

Mumola, C. J., & Karberg, J. C. (2006). *Drug use and dependence, state & federal prisoners, 2004.* Washington, DC: Bureau of Justice Statistics.

Murphy, J. G. (1973). Marxism and retribution. *Philosophy & Public Affairs,* 217–243.

Office of the Inspector General. (2010). *A review of federal prison industries' electronic-waste recycling program.* Washington, DC: US Department of Justice. Retrieved from https://oig.justice.gov/reports/BOP/o1010.pdf

Office of the Inspector General. (2015). *Streamline: Measuring its effect on illegal border crossing.* Washington, DC: US Department of Homeland Security.

Pratt, T. C. (2009). *Addicted to incarceration: Corrections policy and the politics of misinformation in the United States.* Thousand Oaks, CA: Sage.

Raza, A. E. (2011). Legacies of the racialization of incarceration: From convict-lease to the prison industrial complex. *Journal of the Institute of Justice and International Studies, 11,* 159–170.

Roth, M. P. (2006). Chain gangs. In *Prisons and prison systems: A global encyclopedia* (pp. 56–67). Westport, CT: Greenwood Press.

Sentencing Project. (2015). *Trends in U.S. corrections.* Washington, DC: Author. Retrieved from http://sentencingproject.org/doc/publications/inc_Trends_in_Corrections_Fact_sheet.pdf

Spohn, C., & Sample, L. L. (2013). The dangerous drug offender in federal court: Intersections of race, ethnicity, and culpability. *Crime & Delinquency, 59*(1), 3–31.

Steffensmeier, D., & Demuth, S. (2000). Ethnicity and sentencing outcomes in US federal courts: Who is punished more harshly? *American Sociological Review, 65*(5), 705–729.

Stumpf, J. P. (2011). Doing time: Crimmigration law and the perils of haste. *UCLA Law Review, 58,* 1705–1748.

Thompson, H. A. (2012). The prison industrial complex: A growth industry in a shrinking economy. *New Labor Forum, 21*(3), 38–47.

Tinto, E. A. (2001). The role of gender and relationship in reforming the Rockefeller Drug Laws. *New York University Law Review, 76*(3), 906–944.

Travis, J., Western, B., & Redburn, S. (Eds.). (2014). *The growth of incarceration in the United States: Exploring causes and consequences.* Washington, DC: National Academies Press.

Urbina, I. (2009, March 27). Despite red flags, judges ran kickback scheme for years. *New York Times.* Retrieved from http://www.nytimes.com/2009/03/28/us/28judges.html?_r=3&

Walker, S. (2001). *Sense and nonsense about crime and drugs: A policy guide* (5th ed.). Belmont, CA: Wadsworth.

Wehr, K., & Aseltine, E. (2013). *Beyond the prison industrial complex: Crime and incarceration in the 21st century.* New York, NY: Routledge.

Wood, Philip J. (2007) Globalization and prison privatization. *International Political Sociology, 1*(3), 222–239.

COPYRIGHTED MATERIAL — DO NOT DUPLICATE, DISTRIBUTE, OR POST

COPYRIGHTED MATERIAL — DO NOT DUPLICATE, DISTRIBUTE, OR POST

COPYRIGHTED MATERIAL — DO NOT DUPLICATE. DISTRIBUTE. OR POST

COPYRIGHTED MATERIAL — DO NOT DUPLICATE, DISTRIBUTE, OR POST

MASS INCARCERATION AND HOW IT AFFECTS PRISON CULTURE AND ITS OPERATIONS

6

LIZA CHOWDHURY, PhD

Reading Objectives

- Know the ethical issues surrounding mass incarceration
- Understand the influence of politics and the war on drugs
- Become familiar with disparate criminal justice outcomes and their effects
- Understand how inmate subculture promotes violence and corruption
- Recognize the critical issues surrounding solitary confinement

---

OVERVIEW

The United States leads the world in incarcerating its citizens. The fundamental themes of life, liberty, and the pursuit of happiness have been overshadowed by the overrepresentation of **marginalized communities** housed in our current prison system. Recent notable publications have unmasked the several issues within our present-day justice structure. In the book *Just Mercy*, Bryan Stevenson (2014) poignantly asserts that the opposite of poverty is not wealth—it is actually justice. Michelle Alexander's (2012) book *The New Jim Crow* provides proof as to how systemic discrimination of people of color has aided in the creation of legal discrimination by our justice system. Radley Balko's (2013) *Rise of the Warrior Cop* chronicles the enabling of brute force used by the police as a result of the fear of crime and the war waged on drug offenders that has been fueled by political pressures since the Nixon era. As a result of the push to overpolice, overincarcerate, and overpunish for the past 3 decades, prison populations have tripled, families have been torn apart, and communities have become broken.

Beyond the communities affected by **mass incarceration**, a system overused to house offenders has also suffered the consequences of the **crime control model**. The prison boom of the 1990s placed several pressures on the capabilities of state correctional systems, has exhausted state budgets, and has had harmful effects on marginalized communities (Clear, 2007; Jacobson, 2006). These effects are typically felt by communities of color in urban America that are plagued with issues that range from poor health care, insufficient educational systems, lack of employment opportunities, poverty, and high crime rates (Travis & Christiansen, 2006). Mass incarceration has added to the multitude of problems these communities already faced.

The large presence of people of color represented in the prison population is frequently documented by researchers (Tonry, 1995; Morgan & Smith,

45

COPYRIGHTED MATERIAL — DO NOT DUPLICATE, DISTRIBUTE, OR POST

COPYRIGHTED MATERIAL — DO NOT DUPLICATE, DISTRIBUTE, OR POST

2008). Statistics indicate that there is a disproportionate involvement of minorities in the criminal justice system. Based on recent census data, African Americans represent 12% of the U.S. population. However, at all stages in the criminal justice system, whether it be arrest, prosecution, or prison, they have the highest percentage of representation among all racial/ethnic groups. Approximately 50% of all prisoners are Black, 30% are White, and 17% Hispanic (Brewer & Heitzeg, 2008). Along with the prison boom, another phenomenon affecting the prison system is the growing number of female commitments. Whereas the adult male prison population has tripled in the past 20 years, the number of women incarcerated has increased tenfold during the same time span. Women represent the fastest growing sector of the prison population. More than 90,000 prisoners are women, and they are overwhelmingly women of color. African American women are more likely than Hispanic and White women to be in prison. Many women are in prison serving time for nonviolent offenses, especially for drugs (Carson and Golinelli, 2013).

One of the most important controversies in criminal justice and criminology today focuses on whether there is **disparate treatment** of racial and ethnic minorities by decision-making authorities in the criminal justice system (Morgan & Smith, 2008). The overrepresentation of minorities in crime statistics helps support the idea that minorities are more involved with criminality. However, research finds that significant gaps, especially with regard to race and social class, remain between self-report surveys and criminal involvement and official arrest statistics (Morenoff, 2005; Ousey & Lee, 2008). These findings make it difficult to conclude that people of color are more criminally involved than their White counterparts. Rather, entry into prison is in part socially determined by differential exposure to police surveillance, increases in the likelihood of charges resulting in convictions, differences in sentencing patterns, and a host of other structural factors (Beckett, Nyrop, & Pfingst, 2006). The high rates of incarceration of African Americans are a result of disparate outcomes at various levels of interaction with the criminal justice system. Researchers have found that police are more likely to arrest and profile racial and ethnic minorities,

criminal courts proceedings have resulted in racial and ethnic biases that result in racial and ethnic minorities being denied or unable to afford bail, and the lack of resources to hire non–court appointed attorneys have ultimately resulted in receiving more severe sentences (Robinson, 2002).

For the past 30 years, our country has used the criminal justice system as a tool to solve problems such as mental illness, poverty, drug abuse, and social disorganization. As a consequence of the heightened concern for violent crime and the political rhetoric of the 1980s, we are dealing with a system of **punitiveness** that has built fortresslike structures to help solve the "crime problem." We have locked away generations of people and housed them in institutions that are ill prepared to address their needs and truly "correct" them. There are currently 1.6 million people incarcerated in state and federal prisons (Carson, 2014). More than half of the state prison population is incarcerated due to violent offenses (54%), and a large majority has been incapacitated due to nonviolent drug and property offenses. Ninety-three percent of the prison population is made up of men, although the population of women (7%) is growing. Forty percent of state inmates report not completing their high school education. **Recidivism** rates analyzed with 1990s data showed that 44% of inmates are rearrested within the first year of release (Langan & Levin, 2002). Mauer and King (2007) report that the prison demographics shed light on the fact that inmates are predominantly people of color from low socioeconomic backgrounds, and the disparity in the prison populations can be due to the fact that many of these inmates come from disadvantaged areas that are overpoliced.

Supporters of **tough-on-crime policies** argue that the rising prison population is a small consequence compared to the need to protect society and enhance public safety (Balko, 2013). Perhaps some crimes have been prevented due to the rise in incarceration rates, but some criminologists argue that communities with higher prison growth do not always have comparable drops in crime (Tonry, 2011). It is imperative to understand how our current sentencing practices have aided in the various problems faced by our corrections system. There was a time in our country that we took a more rehabilitative approach to crime. Prior to the 1960s, the

COPYRIGHTED MATERIAL — DO NOT DUPLICATE, DISTRIBUTE, OR POST

COPYRIGHTED MATERIAL — DO NOT DUPLICATE, DISTRIBUTE, OR POST

medical model dictated how we treated drug and alcohol addictions. The focus of treatment, compassion, and tolerance outweighed the current war on drugs approach (Balko, 2013). The addict was looked at as a person who needed medical intervention and treatment. Martinson's (1974) "What Works? Questions and Answers About Prison Reform"—better known as the "Nothing Works" report—was transformative in refuting the effectiveness of rehabilitation. Shifting from treating to incarcerating became a political trend. Being tough on crime and criminalizing drug offenders became a winning political strategy for liberal and conservative politicians. As a result, politicians acted on their promises of public safety by enacting tough-on-crime bills, increasing spending on incarceration and law enforcement, and making sure that punishment was inflicted on those who broke the law. Some results of this "just deserts" retributive and crime control model of dealing with offenders have been the tripling of the prison population since 1987, an increase in spending from $10 billion in spending to about $60 billion in spending, and high recidivism rates of those who are released from prisons and enter the community. With such a large investment in public safety, the hope was to yield high success rates to help "correct" clients, but instead, we have created institutions that have just become social control mechanisms to control members of society that have already been plagued by structural disadvantages.

Central to a critical understanding of minorities in corrections is sentencing, particularly disparities in race, ethnicity, and class, as well as gender. Since the 1980s the political push for tougher sentencing and crime control pushed legislators to create tougher sentencing acts. Drug users and sellers were portrayed as being evil by media propaganda. Truth-in-sentencing laws were created, three-strikes laws were created, **determinate sentencing** was instilled, **zero-tolerance policing** became practiced, **mandatory minimums** for drug offenses were created, and sentencing guidelines became established in both federal and state courts (Balko, 2013; Alexander, 2012). The original goals were to reduce disparity in sentencing for similar criminal violations, reduce prison **overcrowding**, and make sentences more rational. The guidelines were

created to help judges have a more prescribed way of how to punish offenders (Clear, Reisig, & Cole, 2012). However, despite the hopes for reforms, a major change occurred in the processing of cases in the U.S. criminal justice system. The power of discretion in terms of sentencing transferred from the judge to the prosecutor. The ability of prosecutors to choose the charge and to plea bargain has affected the accused. A common practice in the U.S. justice system is that the accused sometimes pleads guilty and cooperates in order to avoid the harsh sentences specified for some crimes. A new assembly-line format of the criminal justice system has thus been created as a result of plea bargaining and overclogged court calendars, and an overpopulated corrections system has become the result of the new sentencing policies and criminal justice practices. Criminologists have questioned the ethics and credibility of a system that has relied on incarceration as a problem-solving tool. Questionability in the integrity of prisons sheds light on the disparity in prison populations, the practice of overcriminalizing nonviolent offenses, and the emphasis on tough-on-crime initiatives that have allowed prison populations to soar. As a result, we are currently faced with a system that has a difficult time "correcting" its inmates.

OVERCROWDING AND ITS CONSEQUENCES

Once a person is incarcerated, prison hardships include overcrowding, unaddressed mental health issues, poor health care, high risk of HIV, gang violence, lack of programming, and lack of effective therapeutic programs. All of these issues pose obstacles for prison administrators and prison inmates. Significant numbers of inmates have substance-abuse problems and usually serve time for nonviolent drug-related offenses. Policy experts claim that many are in prison due to the war on drugs policies that have a disproportionate impact on people of color (Welch, 2013). In their research, Hochstetler, Murphy, and Simons (2004) found that most prisoners come from disadvantaged backgrounds, which resulted in few resources, and were plagued by several problems before they began their prison sentences. For most prisoners, the challenges

COPYRIGHTED MATERIAL — DO NOT DUPLICATE, DISTRIBUTE, OR POST

COPYRIGHTED MATERIAL — DO NOT DUPLICATE, DISTRIBUTE, OR POST

of incarceration, coupled with their personal and family issues and limitations, increase their problems and lead to a poor prison adjustment.

Society has several myths about prison culture based on Hollywood depictions of prison life. Popular shows such as *Oz* and *Orange Is the New Black* shed light on the several problems faced by inmates once incarcerated, but despite the glamorization of prisons in popular culture, it is important to understand prison is a society within itself and that there are several pains associated with incarceration, which are a result of the conditions of confinement. Inmates create functioning communities that have values, roles, and customs, and they sometimes have leadership structures or form cliques for protection and identity. Several researchers have studied prison subcultures. The work of Sykes and Messinger (1960) on prison indicates that prison culture arises due to **deprivation** and the pains of incarceration. Some pains of incarceration include goods, autonomy, freedom, and relationships. The alternative viewpoint by Irwin and Cressey (1962) is that inmate communities are brought in from outside influences or a product of **importation** from the free society. Some ways that inmates adapt to prison are either by "**doing time**," "**gleaning**," "**jailing**," or by becoming a "**disorganized criminal**."

"Doing time" means that inmates look at their role as a prisoner as a consequence of their criminal career, and they do their time by adapting to the inmate code. Inmates that "glean" participate in prison programs to improve themselves so they can reintegrate to society once they have completed their sentence. The inmates who "jail" break ties with their social support systems outside their prison and conform to the culture of institutionalization. They begin to take on roles of leadership in order to gain power in prison politics. "Disorganized criminals" have the toughest time adapting to prison, and this may be due to the fact that they have physical or mental disabilities. These adaptive roles are what helps some inmates survive in prison. Due to the lack of goods, resources, and contact with the free world, their success or failure can depend on how they adjust to prison life. Sykes and Messinger (1960) highlighted in their work that the inmate code emphasizes the importance of toughness and not trusting guards. A life of deprivation of

goods and living based on humble means are a part of punishment. As a consequence, underground prison economies have been created to supplement the lack of resources found in prisons.

Along with adapting to the world of captivity, inmates also desire goods and services from the outside, but part of punishment involves being deprived of everything. Recognizing that prisoners do have some needs that are not met, prisons have a commissary, or "store," from which residents may periodically purchase a limited number of items—toilet articles, tobacco, snack foods, and other items—in exchange for credits drawn on their accounts. The size of an inmate's account varies. Inmates have a formal prison store for a limited number goods, but an informal underground economy also exists. A life of extreme simplicity is part of the punishment, and correctional administrators believe that to maintain discipline and security, rules must be enforced and all prisoners must be treated alike so none can gain higher position, status, or comfort levels because of wealth or access to goods. Prisoners are deprived of nearly everything but bare necessities. Their diet and routine are monotonous, and their recreational opportunities are limited. They experience a loss of identity (because of uniformity of treatment) and lack of responsibility. Some of the goods and services found in the underground prison economy are things that the inmates are deprived of, such as sex, drugs, alcohol, and food. A bartering system has been developed in the underground prison economy to continue the flow of goods and services not found in the prison commissary. **Contraband** are things that are prohibited within the prison, but these items thrive in the underground economy in prison because of their prohibition. These transactions can lead to violence if debt is unpaid or goods are stolen. Periodic lockdowns and cell sweeps may help disrupt the prison economy by confiscating contraband, but goods continue to get smuggled into prison.

Ethical issues are raised when deciphering how these goods come into prison. Prison guards are faced with temptations of participating in illegal prison contraband smuggling as a result of a thriving underground prison economy. In 2015 several prison guards in the Philadelphia prison system were indicted on charges of delivering OxyContin

COPYRIGHTED MATERIAL — DO NOT DUPLICATE, DISTRIBUTE, OR POST

COPYRIGHTED MATERIAL — DO NOT DUPLICATE, DISTRIBUTE, OR POST

pills, cell phones, and other goods in exchange for cash payments (Smith & Chang, 2015). Cases like this are not new and continue to be an issue within the prison system.

VIOLENCE IN PRISON AND PRISON RIOTS

It is important to note that with the rise of mass incarceration, violence within prisons also became commonplace. Prisons breed a recipe for a hostile environment because of their coercive nature and housing of offenders with various social problems. Several studies have found that this type of punitive environment also raises safety concerns for guards. Jefferis's (1994) study found that more than half of the corrections officers in his study had been physically assaulted during the duration of their career. Camp and Camp (1993) discovered that assaults by inmates on staff were commonplace in prisons. Some assaults may occur when guards break up fights among inmates, some are carefully planned attacks on guards, and others occur when guards approach emotionally unstable prisoners (Light, 1991). However, researchers have found that the safety of correctional officers rests in the hands of prison administrators. Administrators must invest in training and the improvement of facilities so that they create a safer and more humane environment for both guards and inmates (Useem & Reisig, 1999; Crews & Montgomery, 2002).

The use of force by officials against inmates remains a controversial issue. In 2014 the *New Yorker* magazine did an extensive exposé about an ex–Riker's Island inmate named Kalief Browder. His accounts of his stay at Riker's Island exposed the extent of the violence, abuse, sexual assault, and overuse of solitary confinement by our current corrections system. The most shocking revelation was that Browder was a juvenile and had never even been found guilty of his charge of allegedly stealing a book bag. A surveillance video from within the facility was released soon after that clearly supported the allegations made by this young man. The video shows a guard escorting a teenage Browder handcuffed out of his cell and knocking him to the ground and several minutes of the guard and other guards attacking Kalief. A young activist, Browder

spent a few years in his young adult life to continue to raise awareness about the pains he faced while incarcerated and waiting for trial (Haney, Weill, Bakhshay, & Lockett, 2015). However, in 2015 Browder—this young man who spent his teenage years incarcerated for a crime that he was never found guilty of—committed suicide. His story led to several policy changes, which included the ban of the use of solitary confinement for juveniles at Riker's Island, and nationwide attention was placed on juvenile justice reform.

Prison staff use of force can be divided into two categories, official and unofficial. **Official force** can be used if there is a dangerous situation that involves the risk of life or property within the facility. Administrators support the use of force because some find it necessary to maintain control. Several years prior to Browder's incarceration, Riker's Island was under scrutiny in 1986 due to a riot with alleged excessive use of force by guards. Several recommendations were made that discussed the need to regulate the use-of-force policy and create a more positive jail environment (Welch, 2013). Marquart (1986) explained that **unofficial force** is used to instill fear and subordination in inmates by the prison staff. *Hudson v. McMillian* ruled that when officers maliciously and sadistically assault inmates, inmates' rights are violated, and this is cruel and unusual punishment.

Scholars have proposed some solutions to help in the issue of violence in prison. Zupan (1991) focused on the importance of prison design by encouraging safer and humane environments. Dilulio (1987) proposed that prisons can become safer if more civility and justice were promoted within the prisons. Many scholars have promoted the use of rehabilitative ideology and effective prison programs as a way of managing prisons instead of enforcing the custodial ideology. In 2015 Facebook CEO Mark Zuckerberg made a visit to one of the country's most notorious prisons, San Quentin. His visit was to shed light on the importance of reforming our current criminal justice system. Although San Quentin was once notoriously known for its prison violence and riots, in recent years the prison has allowed innovative programming, which includes computer coding programs, yoga, and college education. The prison now boasts the

COPYRIGHTED MATERIAL — DO NOT DUPLICATE, DISTRIBUTE, OR POST

COPYRIGHTED MATERIAL — DO NOT DUPLICATE, DISTRIBUTE, OR POST

nation's lowest number of inmates returning to their prison due to recidivism. This example of shifting from a **custodial model** to a more **rehabilitative model** has proved successful in San Quentin.

PRISON INFRACTIONS AND THE USE OF SOLITARY CONFINEMENT

Researchers have found that poor prison adjustment has harmful effects on inmate rehabilitation and reintegration in the community once the inmate is released. Some experts view incapacitation and rehabilitation as two sides of the same coin; others favor coercive control over rehabilitation or vice versa. In their research, Lynch and Sabol (2001) comment on the tension that exists in the policy-making environment between the two camps: those who favor coercive control and those who continue to stress the importance of rehabilitation opportunities. Lynch and Sabol explain that these two ideology camps affect how law enforcement agents approach the application of standard operating procedures, prisoner needs, and problems while maintaining discipline and order in the prisons.

Research has found that prisoners' socioeconomic factors are associated with their experience with prison adjustment. These factors include age, education, employment, and economic background. Education is a prominent predictor of prisoner adjustment and experience while incarcerated. Higher education attainment is related with less depression and anxiety while in prison.

Prisoners more likely to cause disciplinary infractions include those who are younger and have a low education attainment, such as a high school degree. Also, prisoners who have a history of unemployment, belong to low economic strata, and live in an urban area are more prone to causing disciplinary issues. Prisoners who have a prior experience with being incarcerated are also found to be more prone to disciplinary issues. Among prisoners, those who have a history of unemployment were also found to be associated with experiencing distress and other problems and being prone to assault while adjusting into the prison (Porporino & Zamble, 1984).

Haney (2003, 2006) states that prison environments, particularly the negative elements, affect the prison adjustment process. The painful prison environment can cause the prisoner to be affected in such a manner that they become carriers of negative actions and transfer their consequences into the community in which they are released. Through his earlier work, Haney (2003) offered the insight that, for a repeat offender, prison environment brings back the past experiences to memory. In this way, prisoners are not only faced with the issues in their immediate physical environment, they are also dealing with the psychological effects of past incarcerations.

Policies designed by state and federal governments have led to an increase in the prison population. Legal tools such as the three-strikes laws, which augment the likelihood and period of incarceration at the federal and state levels (26 out of 50 states), have contributed to the increase in prison population. This propensity for mass incarceration in the United States has brought the purpose of incarceration into question. The departure from focusing on rehabilitation and the increased use of crime control and mass incarceration have helped foster prison systems that become breeding grounds for inhumane treatment of prisoners (Welch, 2013). This policy framework, which has led to an increase in prison population, has rendered many correctional officers less interested in interfering with prisoner factions and gangs and responding to prisoner disciplinary issues with rehabilitative solutions. A rehabilitative solution approach is more focused on addressing the cause of conflict than disciplinary action that matches the disciplinary infraction (Haney, 2003). Correctional officers are the street-level bureaucrats (Maynard-Moody & Musheno, 2003) who are directly responsible for implementing policies related to the criminal justice system. They are important to constructing an understanding of the shape and scope of the penal-harm approach adopted with prisoners and how that changes in different policy environments (Vuolo & Kruttschnitt, 2008). Generally, a prisoner's disciplinary segregation status is used to limit involvement in educational and vocational programs offered in the prisons.

COPYRIGHTED MATERIAL — DO NOT DUPLICATE, DISTRIBUTE, OR POST

COPYRIGHTED MATERIAL — DO NOT DUPLICATE, DISTRIBUTE, OR POST

The process of adjustment into the prison may affect a prisoner's life after incarceration. Studies have shown that those prisoners who have a difficult time adjusting and have more disciplinary issues within the prison are more likely to be incarcerated again (Gendreau, Little, & Goggin, 1996). On the other hand, studies have found that prison enrichment programs and preservation of family ties decrease the likelihood of reoffending once released (Gerber & Fritsch, 1995; Hairston, 1991). Studies have noted gender differences linked with recidivism. Compared to men, women prisoners suffered a larger loss of visits from family over time; they also had more trouble maintaining contact with their children. As a result, women inmates are more susceptible to suffering a loss in their emotional and mental well-being (Koban, 1983; Fogel, 1993; Fogel, Martin, Anderson, Murphy, & Dickson, 1992). The studies reviewed in this section reveal that extreme punishments, the lack of family contact, and the lack of effective treatment in prisons are precursors to why some inmates recidivate.

SOLITARY CONFINEMENT

The types of sanctions that can be administered to inmates can range from the change of work assignment to segregation from the rest of the prison population, which is also known as solitary confinement. **Solitary confinement** is one of the harshest sanctions used in the prison system. There are several reasons why there must be more research about the use of solitary confinement. Recent media reports and research have highlighted the harmful effects of long periods of social isolation. Penal history has also shown that the long-term isolation of inmates resulted in several human rights concerns and recorded incidents of enhanced mental illness, depression, and poor prison adjustment. Grassian and Friedman (1986) report that an extended term in solitary confinement can make prisoners more likely to develop a whole range of adverse psychological reactions that are associated with long periods of isolation.

One of the first mentions of the practice of solitary confinement is found 200 years ago. Quakers introduced the penitentiary system as a means for inmates to have self-reflection and perform penance in isolation (Vasiliades, 2005). Adhering to this ideology, the practice of solitary confinement gave the prisoner an opportunity to reflect on the offense and be reformed. Quakers used solitary confinement as a tool for prison management and rehabilitation. However, despite the hopes for reform and rehabilitation, the Quakers observed several adverse effects of prolonged isolation. Rather than reforming, the Quakers realized, solitary confinement resulted in many prisoners becoming mentally ill. Also, their prison system was criticized for being too expensive and not being effective, as their methods did not reduce the number of people committing crimes. As a result, by the late 19th century, most countries did not continue the practice of solitary confinement (Shalev, 2008).

In light of these historical findings about the detrimental effect of solitary confinement, it is questionable that modern-day correctional facilities and the penal system have reinstituted this tool of managing and controlling inmates (Vasiliades, 2005). Modern-day segregation units encompass a specific prison area, known in the most up-to-date maximum-security facilities as secure housing units (Vasiliades, 2005). Researchers have found that the overuse of solitary confinement today is due to many factors. These factors include the overcrowding of prisons due to the war on drugs and legislative policies that require longer sentence lengths, mandatory sentencing, strict sentencing guidelines for minor offenses, younger and more violent inmates, and insufficient funding for proper security (Welch, 2013).

There are several physical and psychological harms affiliated with solitary confinement. Historical and modern research documents that physiological harms associated with long periods of segregation include deterioration of eyesight, insomnia, heart palpitations, lethargy, and several other symptoms. Psychological harms include anxiety, depression, anger, cognitive disturbances, self-harm, suicide, hallucinations, paranoia, and psychosis. Research has also uncovered that prior history of medical or psychological disorders can become aggravated by being in solitary confinement (Cloyes, Lovell, Allen, & Rhodes, 2006; Haynie, 2003; Grassian, 2006).

COPYRIGHTED MATERIAL — DO NOT DUPLICATE, DISTRIBUTE, OR POST

COPYRIGHTED MATERIAL — DO NOT DUPLICATE, DISTRIBUTE, OR POST

There are several reasons why solitary confinement continues to be used in modern-day prisons. The reasons include punishment, protection, prison management, national security, pretrial investigation, and the lack of other institutional solutions. In regard to use of solitary confinement as a sanction, it is considered the highest form of punishment for committing the most egregious prison offense. It is also used as a prison management technique to isolate inmates who are considered potentially violent, disruptive, and gang related (Shalev, 2008). Although solitary confinement is a convenient tool used in prison to isolate prisoners to prevent disruptions, violence, and infractions, there have been inconsistent findings regarding its effectiveness (Shalev, 2008). Therefore, legal safeguards and constant reviews of those in isolation are necessary so that Eighth Amendment protections against cruel and unusual punishment are not violated.

Solitary confinement is a very controversial punishment that has been historically documented for its harmful effects and challenges relating to cruel and unusual punishment. In a landmark ruling by the state of California in 2015, the state determined that there would be a change in its use of solitary confinement after a class action suit that charged the state with having over 3,000 inmates in solitary confinement, many of them for indefinite periods. One of the research questions in the field of criminal justice is whether minorities are overrepresented in the current prison population. Also, there is debate surrounding the use of questionable sanctions disproportionately on prisoners of color. Therefore, it is important to develop an understanding of how correctional officers use solitary confinement as a tool and whether it is a tool that is more likely to be used disproportionately on certain inmates than others.

CONCLUSION

There are several reasons why treatment in prisons is an important area of study. The correctional population in the United States is massive, with 1 out of 100 Americans under some sort of correctional supervision, including prison, parole, and probation (Olson, 2013). Treatment inside prison affects psychological well-being, future criminal activity, and recidivism (Chen & Shapiro, 2007; Drago, Galbiati, & Vertova, 2009; Selke, 1993). Incarceration has a disproportionate effect on the minority population (Yates & Fording, 2005; Western, 2006).

In 2015 President Barack Obama made criminal justice reform his top priority. He was the first sitting president ever to visit a correctional facility, and his visit was documented by the VICE network in the form of a documentary called *Fixing the System*. Since then, he has made it his priority to raise awareness on the issues plaguing a broken system that incarcerates a great deal of nonviolent offenders and then shelters them in institutions that have very little capability to help them reintegrate back into society once they return. The issues mentioned in this chapter—such as mass incarceration, disparity in sentencing, overpolicing of targeted communities, lack of opportunities, mental illness, poor health care, poor educational systems, overcrowding, violence, lack of treatment and programming, and the lack of acceptance once back in society—are just a few of the obstacles inmates live with every day. In order to deal with the problems mentioned previously and create a more morally sound and ethical corrections system, research asserts that attention has to be placed on training, better facilities, effective prison programming, investing in poor communities, and the reintegration of ex-offenders.

Discussion Questions

1 What are some of the consequences of mass incarceration?
2 How has overcrowding impacted our prison system?
3 What are some policy suggestions that can help ease the pains of incarceration?

COPYRIGHTED MATERIAL — DO NOT DUPLICATE, DISTRIBUTE, OR POST

COPYRIGHTED MATERIAL — DO NOT DUPLICATE, DISTRIBUTE, OR POST

4 What are some issues related to solitary confinement?

5 How can we reduce prison violence?

6 How can we fix our current system?

REFERENCES

Alexander, M. (2012). *The new Jim Crow: Mass incarceration in the age of colorblindness.* New York: New Press.

Balko, R. (2013). *Rise of the warrior cop: The militarization of America's police forces.* New York: PublicAffairs.

Beckett, K., Nyrop, K., & Pfingst, L. (2006). Race, drugs, and policing: Understanding disparities in drug delivery arrests. *Criminology, 44*(1), 105–137.

Brewer, R. M., & Heitzeg, N. A. (2008). The racialization of crime and punishment criminal justice, color-blind racism, and the political economy of the prison industrial complex. *American Behavioral Scientist, 51*(5), 625–644.

Camp, G. M., & Camp, C. M. (1993). *The Corrections Yearbook, 1993.* New York: Criminal Justice Institute.

Carson, E. A. (2014). *Prisoners in 2013.* Washington, DC: Bureau of Justice Statistics.

Carson, E. A., & Golinelli, D. (2013). *Prisoners in 2012: Trends in admissions and releases, 1991–2012.* Washington, DC: Bureau of Justice Statistics.

Chen, M. K., & Shapiro, J. M. (2007). Do harsher prison conditions reduce recidivism? A discontinuity-based approach. *American Law and Economics Review, 9*(1), 1–29.

Clear, T. R. (2007). *Imprisoning communities: How mass incarceration makes disadvantaged neighborhoods worse.* Oxford: Oxford University Press.

Clear, T. R., Reisig, M., & Cole, G. (2012). *American corrections.* Belmont, CA: Wadsworth.

Cloyes, K. G., Lovell, D., Allen, D. G., & Rhodes, L. A. (2006). Assessment of psychosocial impairment in a supermaximum security unit sample. *Criminal Justice and Behavior, 33*(6), 760–781.

Crews, G., & Montgomery, R. (2002). Prison violence. In D. Levinson (Ed.), *Encyclopedia of crime and punishment* (pp. 1240–1244). Thousand Oaks, CA: Sage

Dilulio, J. (1987). *Governing prisons: A comparative study of prison management.* New York: Free Press.

Drago, F., Galbiati, R., & Vertova, P. (2009). The deterrent effects of prison: Evidence from a natural experiment. *Journal of Political Economy, 117*(2), 257–280.

Fogel, C. I. (1993). Hard T: The stressful nature of incarceration for women. *Issues in Mental Health Nursing, 14*(4), 367–377.

Fogel, C. I., Martin, S. L., Anderson, N. L., Murphy, S. A., & Dickson, L. A. S. (1992). The mental health of incarcerated women. *Western Journal of Nursing Research, 14*(1), 30–47.

Gendreau, P., Little, T., & Goggin, C. (1996). A meta-analysis of the predictors of adult offender recidivism: What works! *Criminology, 34*(4), 575–608.

Gerber, J., & Fritsch, E. J. (1995). Adult academic and vocational correctional education programs: A review of recent research. *Journal of Offender Rehabilitation, 22*(1–2), 119–142.

Grassian, S. (2006). Psychiatric effects of solitary confinement. *Washington University Journal of Law and Policy, 22,* 325–347.

Grassian, S., & Friedman, N. (1986). Effects of sensory deprivation in psychiatric seclusion and solitary confinement. *International Journal of Law and Psychiatry, 8*(1), 49–65.

Hairston, C. F. (1991). Family ties during imprisonment: Important to whom and for what. *Journal of Sociology and Social Welfare, 18*(1), 87–104.

Haney, C. (2003). Mental health issues in long-term solitary and "supermax" confinement. *Crime & Delinquency, 49*(1), 124–156.

Haney, C. (2006). The wages of prison overcrowding: Harmful psychological consequences and dysfunctional correctional reactions. *Washington University Journal of Law and Policy, 22*(1), 265–293.

Haney, C., Weill, J., Bakhshay, S., & Lockett, T. (2015). Examining jail isolation: What we don't know can be profoundly harmful. *Prison Journal,* 0032885515605491.

Haynie, D. (2003). Contexts of risk? Explaining the link between girls' pubertal development and their delinquency involvement. *Social Forces, 82,* 355–397.

Hochstetler, A., Murphy, D. S., & Simons, R. L. (2004). Damaged goods: Exploring predictors of distress in prison inmates. *Crime & Delinquency, 50*(3), 436–457.

COPYRIGHTED MATERIAL — DO NOT DUPLICATE, DISTRIBUTE, OR POST

COPYRIGHTED MATERIAL — DO NOT DUPLICATE, DISTRIBUTE, OR POST

Irwin, J., & Cressey, D. R. (1962). Thieves, convicts and the inmate culture. *Social Problems, 10*(2), 142–155.

Jacobson, M. (2006). Reversing the punitive turn: The limits and promise of current research. *Criminology & Public Policy, 5*(2), 277–284.

Jefferis, E. (1994, September/October). Violence in correctional institutions. *American Jails*, 25–26, 30–32.

Koban, L. A. (1983). Parents in prison: A comparative analysis of the effects of incarceration on the families of men and women. *Research in Law, Deviance and Social Control, 5*, 171–183.

Langan, P. A., & Levin, D. J. (2002). Recidivism of prisoners released in 1994. *Federal Sentencing Reporter, 15*(1), 58–65.

Light, K. C. (1991). Assaults on prison officers: Interactional themes. *Justice Quarterly, 8*(2), 243–262.

Lynch, J. P., & Sabol, W. J. (2001, September 18). *Prisoner reentry in perspective*. Washington, DC: Urban Institute. Retrieved from https://www.urban.org/research/publication/prisoner-reentry-perspective

Marquart, J. W. (1986). Prison guards and the use of physical coercion as a mechanism of prisoner control. *Criminology, 24*(2), 347–366.

Martinson, R. (1974). What works? Questions and answers about prison reform. *Public Interest, 35*(2), 22–54.

Mauer, M., & King, R. S. (2007). *Uneven justice: State rates of incarceration by race and ethnicity*. Washington, DC: Sentencing Project.

Maynard-Moody, S. W., & Musheno, M. C. (2003). *Cops, teachers, counselors: Stories from the front lines of public service*. Ann Arbor: University of Michigan Press.

Morenoff, J. D. (2005). Racial and ethnic disparities in crime and delinquency in the United States. *Ethnicity and Causal Mechanisms*, 139–173.

Morgan, K. D., & Smith, B. (2008). The impact of race on parole decision-making. *Justice Quarterly, 25*(2), 411–435.

Olson, J. (2013). *Social construction and political decision making in the American prison system(s)* (Doctoral dissertation, University of Kentucky).

Ousey, G. C., & Lee, M. R. (2008). Racial disparity in formal social control: An investigation of alternative explanations of arrest rate inequality. *Journal of Research in Crime and Delinquency, 45*(3), 322–355.

Porporino, F. J., & Zamble, E. (1984). Coping with imprisonment. *Canadian Journal of Criminology, 26*, 403.

Robinson, M. B. (2002). *Justice blind?: Ideals and realities of American criminal justice*. Upper Saddle River, NJ: Prentice Hall.

Selke, W. L. (1993). *Prisons in crisis*. Bloomington: Indiana University Press.

Shalev, S. (2008). *A sourcebook on solitary confinement*. London: Author.

Smith, S., & Chang, D. (2015). Prison guards smuggle Oxycontin pills, phones to inmates in exchange for cash: Police. Retrieved from http://www.nbcphiladelphia.com/news/local/Prison-Corruption-Case-Unveiled-325982701.html#ixzz3qRetiI00

Stevenson, B. (2014). *Just mercy: A story of justice and redemption*. New York: Spiegel & Grau.

Sykes, G. M., & Messinger, S. L. (1960). The inmate social system. In R. Cloward, D. R. Cressey, G. H. Grosser, R. McCleery, L. E. Ohlin, G. M. Sykes, & S. L. Messinger (Eds.), *Theoretical studies in social organization of the prison* (pp. 5–19). New York: Social Science Research Council.

Tonry, M. H. (1995). *Malign neglect: Race, crime, and punishment in America* (Vol. 95). New York: Oxford University Press.

Tonry, M. H. (Ed.). (2011). *Why punish? How much?: A reader on punishment*. Oxford: Oxford University Press.

Travis, J., & Christiansen, K. (2006). Failed reentry: The challenges of back-end sentencing. *Georgetown Journal on Poverty Law and Policy, 13*(2), 249–260.

Useem, B., & Reisig, M. D. (1999). Collective action in prisons: Protests, disturbances and riots. *Criminology, 37*(4), 734–760.

Vasiliades, E. (2005). Solitary confinement and international human rights: Why the US prison system fails global standards. *American University International Law Review, 21*(1), 71–99.

Vuolo, M., & Kruttschnitt, C. (2008). Prisoners' adjustment, correctional officers, and context: The foreground and background of punishment in late modernity. *Law & Society Review, 42*(2), 307–336.

Welch, M. (2013). *Corrections: A critical approach*. New York: McGraw-Hill.

Western, B. (2006). *Punishment and inequality in America*. New York: Russell Sage Foundation.

Yates, J., & Fording, R. (2005). Politics and state punitiveness in Black and White. *Journal of Politics, 67*(4), 1099–1121.

Zupan, L. L. (1991). *Jails: Reform and the New Generation philosophy*. Cincinnati: Anderson.

COPYRIGHTED MATERIAL — DO NOT DUPLICATE. DISTRIBUTE. OR POST

COPYRIGHTED MATERIAL — DO NOT DUPLICATE, DISTRIBUTE, OR POST

7 | GENDER AND FAMILY

DOSHIE PIPER, PhD, AND GEORGEN GUERRERO, PhD

Reading Objectives

- Understand how deeply rooted notions of patriarchy shape our understanding of females in criminal justice
- Understand that gender-specific issues do not automatically impose ethical dilemmas
- Differentiate between the terms *ethics of justice and ethics of care*
- Learn the various ethical issues that females face in law enforcement, courts, and corrections

---

OVERVIEW

Some scholars believe that exploring ethics may require evaluating one's core belief system (Braswell, McCarthy, & McCarthy, 2008; Cheeseman, San Miguel, Frantzen, & Nored, 2011). This is a difficult task for most people, because it requires individuals to challenge their existence, integrity, objectivity, standards, and principles about life and all that they thought they knew about them. Taking this already complex idea of ethics and adding another component or two such as gender and the family can further compound the issue. This has a lot to do with the assumptions that we hold about gender, assumptions heavily rooted in patriarchy. Despite the many advances made in society, there still exist male power and domination in society as an influence on females in most aspects of female decision making.

As a result, attempting to make sense of ethical or unethical behavior based on laws or policies from a gendered perspective can be problematic. The problems arise when considerations are not given to females and their relatively recent involvement in criminal justice occupations and the traditional male definition of ethics. Traditionally, males tend to think about morality vertically and base their values in a hierarchy (Menkel-Meadow, 2005). This male mode of reasoning is referred to as the "logic of the ladder," which created an "ethics of justice" (Menkel-Meadow, 2005 p. 275). On the other hand, females opposed the male moral reasoning and adopted moral reasoning based on relationships, contextual to the problem and focused on people, which created the "ethic of care" (Menkel-Meadow, 2005 p. 276).

Regardless of the male "ethics of justice" or the female "ethics of care," females historically did not hold positions in the male-dominated legal field. It was not until the 1960s and 1970s that women showed an increased participation in the workforce (Lilly, Ball, & Cullen, 2015). Adler and Adler (1975), in their writing of *Sisters in Crime*, argued that lifting restrictions on women's opportunities in the marketplace gave them the chance to be

COPYRIGHTED MATERIAL — DO NOT DUPLICATE. DISTRIBUTE. OR POST

COPYRIGHTED MATERIAL — DO NOT DUPLICATE, DISTRIBUTE, OR POST

as greedy, violent, and crime prone as men. This relatively recent rise of women in the workforce now presented an opportunity for females to be subjected to ethical dilemmas.

It is also important to consider that the employment of women in the criminal justice system has been limited. Women have traditionally been shut out of male-dominated occupations such as police, attorneys, and corrections (Mallicoat, 2012). Despite the women's suffrage movement nearly 100 years ago legislative reforms gaining women the right to vote, it was not until the social movements of the 1960s and 1970s that women began to reap the benefits of the women's liberation and enter these occupations. Since their entrance, they have been faced with an overly masculine culture that has made their entry very difficult. The predominantly male workforces in criminal justice have a very rigid perspective that has generally been negative about women being there.

This chapter will explore the ethical impacts of gender and work in criminal justice–related occupations. The chapter will begin with the theoretical considerations of patriarchy and gender discrimination in criminal justice work. Following is a breakdown of gender involvement and ethical considerations in each component of the criminal justice system: police, courts, and corrections. This chapter will conclude with a discussion on the impacts and implication of improving gender equality in criminal justice–related fields.

THEORETICAL CONSIDERATIONS

Females entering the workforce have always been met with opposition. Women have been faced with the challenge of gender roles, with the majority of society viewing a woman's role as being in the home as caretakers. Let's apply this patriarchal view to women who are interested in criminal justice work. Patriarchy would question the motives of females pursing this line of work. It would suggest that women are not capable of being objective and basing decisions on laws and statutes or policies and procedures. Rather, patriarchy would propose that females are emotional and subjective and would base their decisions on how they are feeling as opposed to the rule of law. This

line of thinking has been confirmed in the criminal justice literature. Hagan (1990) wrote about the power-control theory, suggesting that males and females are socialized differently, signifying why males and females pursue different occupations.

Power-control theory predicts that the more patriarchal the family structure, the greater the gender gap in behavior between sons and daughters. Because the gender roles in delinquency are shaped in the family by reflection from the workplace, power-control theory offers a potential explanation of the effect of the changing occupational roles of women. Typical "street criminality," then, is a product of powerlessness for females and lower class, non-White males.

Hagan's (1990) power-control theory, while not a feminist theory, is an integrated theory that is feminist informed. This theory combines a feminist perspective with social-control theory to explain family relationships and to present a power-control theory of gender and delinquency. Hagan (1990) argues that the power relationships in larger society, especially in the workplace, are reflected in the family. The critical components of gender relations are rooted in the patriarchal family, as they relate to delinquent behavior, including the way in which delinquency is defined, the amount and type of control parents exercise over children, and gender preferences for risk taking. Boys are given far more leeway for risk-taking behavior, and that behavior is reinforced by the view of boys being boys. Girls, on the other hand, are shunned for risk-taking behavior, and the behavior is redirected.

GENDER IN LAW ENFORCEMENT

Despite law enforcement being a male-dominated profession, females have had a very strong impact in the criminal justice field through law enforcement. Women have helped shape and transform policing into a more complete and compatible profession for society. Women bring a strong sense of professionalism, integrity, and dedication to the profession.

Across the nation, women make up approximately 9% of all sworn officers. Despite all the negative stereotypes about female officers in policing—such as women should not be police officers,

COPYRIGHTED MATERIAL — DO NOT DUPLICATE, DISTRIBUTE, OR POST

COPYRIGHTED MATERIAL — DO NOT DUPLICATE, DISTRIBUTE, OR POST

women could not handle themselves or the public when needed, the public will not respect them, they will not be able to handle dangerous situations, they will undermine their male partners, and they will get hurt on the job—research has found that women have had a positive impact on policing. Research reveals that none of these general stereotypes are true. In fact, many of these stereotypes are just the opposite of what was once believed about females working in policing.

Even outside of policing, it is generally understood that women are more verbally proficient than men. Women use this ability to effectively communicate in all aspects of the criminal justice system. However, never is it more evident than in policing. Women are able to use their verbal skills to minimize problems with the public and their coworkers, to defuse irate citizens and crisis situations. From an ethical standpoint, female officers bring a greater sense of compassion, sensitivity, and understanding to domestic violence situations. Domestic violence victims are able to speak more freely to female officers than to male officers. Women officers offer greater empathy to policing (Lonsway, Moore, Harrington, Smeal, & Spillar, 2003), and this is invaluable in domestic violence situations.

Additionally, women are credited with being more emotionally and ethically stable than men in their day-to-day activities (Lonsway et al., 2003). Women have been found to have a calming effect on citizens and coworkers. Female officers are less likely to escalate crises or dangerous or even routine situations that they encounter (Lonsway et al., 2003). Women are less likely to use their firearms or escalate to the maximum amount of force allowed in the course of their regular duties. As a result of their verbal proficiency, emotional stability, and their minimal use of their firearms, females receive fewer citizens' complaints, are less likely to injure a citizen during the course of their career, and will actually get injured less than their male counterparts (Lonsway et al., 2003).

As a result of lower rates of injuries, female officers will have less time off and use less sick time than their male counterparts. From an administrative standpoint, it does not matter how great an officer is in his or her duties; if he or she is always on medical leave, then the officer cannot do the job that he or she has been hired to do. As a whole, women officers will take their role as an officer more seriously than their male counterparts and will work attempting to make ethically sound decisions, as if they are trying to prove their value in policing. This is not to argue that we should only hire women in policing, but we should strive to raise the percentage of female officers above 9%. This point is not lost on most agencies across the United States; which continue to aggressively recruit female officers for their departments.

However, there are still areas of concern for women who want to pursue a career in law enforcement. Women, unfortunately, still have to overcome issues of sexual harassment from their male counterparts, administrations, and even the public during their employment. Additionally, female officers are more likely to be subjected to hostility from and negative interactions with their colleagues (Alpert, Dunham, & Stroshine, 2015). Despite great advancements in understanding the dangers of sexual harassment, annual trainings from departments, and repeated attempts to minimize sexual harassment in the workplace, it still exists. Most of the women who work in law enforcement will undoubtedly encounter some level of sexual harassment, from aggressive advancements to occasional innuendos, at some point during the course of their careers. All forms of sexual harassment are by definition unethical and should be avoided in the workplace.

In the past, law enforcement agencies made it very difficult for women to be a part of the workforce. Agencies had "deliberate policies of discrimination and predetermined selection criteria which excluded many women and racial/ethnic minorities" (Alpert et al., 2015, p. 56) from even applying. Many municipal ordinances banned women from patrol assignments. These laws defaulted women in policing to supplementary roles, which limited their opportunities for advancement in rank (Martin & Jurik, 1996). In addition to these local ordinances, many departments had bias-selection criteria. Departments made it almost impossible for females to qualify based on entrance requirements related to education, age, height, weight, agility tests, and veterans' preference (Potts, 1983; Sultan & Townsey, 1981; Martin & Jurik, 1996).

COPYRIGHTED MATERIAL — DO NOT DUPLICATE. DISTRIBUTE. OR POST

COPYRIGHTED MATERIAL — DO NOT DUPLICATE, DISTRIBUTE, OR POST

After many blatant acts of discrimination and disparity in policing, women began to band together and speak up for their constitutional rights. The collective effort of the women's rights movement greatly contributed to the changing stereotype of masculinity and femininity in policing, at least on paper if not in practice. Title VII of the 1964 Civil Rights Act made discrimination based on gender, race, and ethnicity illegal (Alpert et al., 2015). Many law enforcement agencies faced lawsuits for discriminating on the basis of gender.

The Equal Employment Opportunity Commission (EEOC), the governmental agency that enforces federal laws prohibiting discrimination, reveals that another area of concern for female officers is the issue of pregnancy. A large number of complaints to the EEOC each year are related to discrimination practices by employers against pregnant employees. The EEOC prohibits harassment of women as a result of pregnancy, childbirth, or a medical condition related to pregnancy or childbirth.

Another area of concern for the female officer is the inadequacy of general facilities and equipment that is issued to female officers, especially in smaller agencies that may only have one or two female officers within the agency. As a result of policing being a male-dominated profession, many of the facilities that were constructed (in many situations decades ago) were not constructed with the female officer in mind. These facilities may be lacking in gender-separated bathrooms, showers, and locker rooms. Additionally, the uniforms and equipment that are standard issue may not initially have female sizes available, and females are restricted to smaller sized male clothing options.

GENDER IN COURTS

When considering gender and the rule of law and legality, it is important to take into account the historical aspect of women's roles as lawyers. Menkel-Meadow (2005) contributed an article to *Lawyers' Ethics and the Pursuit of Social Justice* examining the role of Portia, a female lawyer in Shakespeare's *The Merchant of Venice* countering the argument of ethical or moral reasoning. The author illustrates the many problems that exist with the traditional ethics of justice as opposed to the ethics of care. The story begins with Portia disguised as a male lawyer appealing on behalf of her client. In this story, she is making a claim for feminist ethics based on equitable, contextual, and merciful sides of the law (Menkel-Meadow, 2005). This play is relevant to gender ethics in the courts because Portia is faced with many modern moral and legal ethical dilemmas, such as contracts, commercial bonds, fidelity, marriage, friendship, loyalty, the spirit versus the letter of the law, justice, legal remedies, and choice (Menkel-Meadow, 2005).

FEMALES AS ATTORNEYS

Let's look at Portia—a woman who was dressed as a man for the sole purpose of practicing law to uncover the ambiguities of gender in the rule of law. The rule of law and the morality of law can be very complex. Answering the question of what is moral and what is just often leads to conflicts. The ethics of care attempts to make decisions in both contexts, and its focus is on harm reduction. In *The Merchant of Venice*, Portia is defending her lover's friend, Antonio, against the demands of Shylock the Jew. The demand is a "pound of flesh" for failure to honor the debt. Portia reasons with Shylock, seeking the feminine side of justice and mercy (Menkel-Meadow, 2005). Shylock is unwavering and sees the law as a source of equal treatment that must be enforced. Portia requests to see the contract of debt and agrees to accommodate Shylock. She reports that Shylock better find a skillful surgeon who can remove the flesh without drawing any blood because blood was not expressed in the bond, only flesh. In this act of savvy lawyering and legal manipulation, Portia has successfully represented her defendant.

This exploration of this Elizabethan Age writing of Shakespeare by Menkel-Meadow (2005) produced much research from the feminist sociologist Cynthia Fuchs Epstein, who suggests that those seeking differences will find them. After studying women lawyers for decades, Epstein (1988) discovered that those who truly seek to establish women's equality with men will find more overlap among the two genders than differences. Additionally, Epstein (1988) maintains that there may be more similarity across gender in legal behavior as opposed to within

COPYRIGHTED MATERIAL — DO NOT DUPLICATE, DISTRIBUTE, OR POST

COPYRIGHTED MATERIAL — DO NOT DUPLICATE, DISTRIBUTE, OR POST

gender. Defense attorneys of both genders seek to mediate the forces in law, calling for the tempering of justice and mercy, appealing to the judge or the jurors. Further studies of lawyers show that women and men are entering the profession for the same reasons. There is very little difference in motivational factors influencing students' entrance into law school (Epstein, 1988).

FEMALES AS DEFENDANTS

During the sentencing phase of the judicial system, we can see a huge disparity in the sentences that are being dealt to female offenders when compared to male offenders. Women tend to receive substantially less time for equal crimes. For example, when averaged out, women receive 60-month sentences for murder, while males receive 80 months for that same offense (Bureau of Justice Statistics, 1999). As another example, female pedophiles will generally receive probation for their crimes, despite the general societal consensus that pedophiles should be incarcerated and kept away from children. However, males hardly ever receive probation for a sexual offense against a child.

Another more general disparity can be seen when examining the differences in crime rates with punishment rates. Women commit approximately 23% of all crime but only make up about 11% of the jail population and 6% of the prison population (Uniform Crime Reports, 2002). When interpreting the inverse, this means that despite the fact that men only constitute 77% of the total crime rate, they account for 89% of the jail population and 94% of the U.S. prison population. From an ethical standpoint, these numbers indicate that women are not being held accountable for their offenses against society in the equivalent manner as men. The legal system is being unethical in its application of the law, in the sentencing of offenders, and in the disparity of those sentences.

CORRECTIONS

In a correctional sense, women are faced with several issues that men generally do not have to face during their incarcerations. Even though many of the prison experiences that women encounter are similar to men's experiences, many are unique to the female gender. Females will encounter the same deprivations, or "pains," of imprisonment that traditionally are associated with incarceration, such as "the deprivation of liberty, the deprivation of goods and services, the deprivation of heterosexual relationships, the deprivation of autonomy, and the deprivation of security" (Sykes, 1958, pp. 63–83).

Females, like their male counterparts, suffer from the inability to move freely in the institutional environment; they are restricted by their institutional counterparts, known as the keepers. Their liberty is deprived by not being able to see their loved ones, specifically their family and friends. They are restricted in the goods and services that are afforded to them at the institution or what is allowed to be delivered and accepted into the institution. They are removed from the possibilities of having heterosexual relationships and moved away from individualism, self-expression, and their own individual security. All institutions thrive on this lack of individualism, restricted access, and ensuring that these pains are met, regardless if the institution is serving a male or female clientele.

It has been thoroughly documented that prisons operate under give-and-take relationships (Sykes, 1958). Officers allow inmates to violate minor rules as long as they do not violate major rules, while inmates allow officers to hold them accountable for major rule violations as long as they do not harass them for every single minor rule violation (Sykes, 1958). Every day, officers allow inmates to engage in minor rule violations; however, an officer could easily wait for an opportune moment to decide to uphold all of the prison's rules and break the unwritten code of allowing minor infractions to go unpunished. A minor disciplinary infraction can have serious consequences in prison, resulting in anything from loss of good time served to solitary confinement or the loss of a special privilege. This give-and-take relationship (that is built on an unethical foundation) in the prison environment provides for a special problem in both male and female prisons. It argues that all behavior from the officer and the inmate can be controlled through a bartering system.

Unfortunately, as a result of this bartering system, the unethical and sexually driven male or female officer has nearly unlimited opportunities to

COPYRIGHTED MATERIAL — DO NOT DUPLICATE, DISTRIBUTE, OR POST

COPYRIGHTED MATERIAL — DO NOT DUPLICATE, DISTRIBUTE, OR POST

engage in unethical sexual solicitations, advancements, and control over the incarcerated. To make matters worse, the inmate does not have many avenues of escape in prison. The inmate is, by all accounts, at the mercy of his or her abuser. The inmate is restricted in his or her movements by prison officials in the prison, can be severely punished or retaliated against for not agreeing to the sexual advancements, will not have a fair grievance procedure at his or her disposal, is unable to defend him- or herself from the officer, and will generally have an unsympathetic public (Law Library, n.d.).

Despite all of their similarities, there are several areas of concern that incarcerated females need address that men do not even have to encounter. As a simple example, approximately 4% to 9% of all women in prison are pregnant. The issue of trying to figure out the proper route of incarceration for these women and their children produces numerous ethical challenges for prison administrators. Administrators are forced to reexamine even the simplest issues, such as determining the appropriate housing assignment. The prison administrator could incarcerate the pregnant inmate in the general population, a special solo housing assignment, or possibly even with other pregnant inmates. Prison administrators are always concerned with prison safety, and the safety of an unborn child produces special considerations. In addition to housing assignments, another issue for the prison administration to quickly address is the determination of the appropriate dietary modifications for the inmate and the unborn child. To allow for proper fetal development, the pregnant inmate will need a variety of extra meal accommodations for her child.

The last—and quite possibly the biggest—issue to be addressed with a pregnant inmate is what to do with the child once it is born. There are several options for the prison system to examine. The most common are to allow the child to be released to a family member until the mother completes her term, to allow the child to be put up for adoption, or to allow the child to remain with the mother for a certain amount of time while incarcerated. The time to consider can be anywhere from a few days up to a couple of years.

Although the final option of having the child stay in prison with the mother is often the most controversial one, it may actually be the best option for all parties involved. The child is able to grow and develop with the mother during the most crucial years of child development. The child is able to bond, attach to the mother, and even breast-feed to allow for optimal child nourishment and development. The mother is able to establish a bond with the child early in their relationship, which will help their relationship grow once she is released. The bonding with the child could help with rehabilitative efforts. The mother could start to understand the importance of making good decisions to avoid being reincarcerated and avoid being taken away from her child or even having the child taken away from her. From the administrative standpoint, allowing the child to stay with the mother could prove to be a valuable behavioral mechanism in prison. An incarcerated mother with a child would more than likely not want to engage in any behavior that could result in having the child taken away from her and would likely avoid any behavior that would put the child's life at risk.

In addition to these issues, there are several natural biological issues that need to be addressed in women's prisons. Women need yearly gynecological examinations and routine access to sanitary napkins. These may appear to be simple issues, but even with smaller prisons that hold approximately 500 inmates, that would break down to approximately two gynecological visits per weekday and countless numbers of sanitary napkins for a whole year for the entire institution. It goes without saying that not all of the women incarcerated will undergo their annual examinations and that the institution would set up certain days for appointments, but even this organized and routine scheduling requires an enhancement of additional security measures and cost for the female institution that is not required at the male institution. From an ethical standpoint, these issues revolve around ensuring that appointments are set and supplies are well stocked throughout the year. Ethically, the administration and the officers need to ensure that the inmate has full access to these appointments and supplies. An unethical officer could easily withhold supplies or cause a disruption to the inmate's scheduling and restrict access to appointments.

Even though males and females both have visitation opportunities for friends and family members,

COPYRIGHTED MATERIAL — DO NOT DUPLICATE, DISTRIBUTE, OR POST

COPYRIGHTED MATERIAL — DO NOT DUPLICATE, DISTRIBUTE, OR POST

as the primary caregiver of the children, females carry an extra burden of not being able to provide for their children while incarcerated. The opportunity to spend time, even if only for a few hours a week, with a child can have a very positive impact on an incarcerated female, especially for the young, first-time inmate who has a strong attachment to her children. From an ethical standpoint, every effort should be made to ensure not only that mothers have access to their children, but also that children have access to their mothers. The power given to officers to approve or deny visits has an enormous impact on the lives of the women who are incarcerated and their children.

The effects that incarceration has on the mother and the child cannot be dismissed. Children could become frightened or traumatized by seeing their mothers incarcerated for the first time. Maybe with longer or multiple visits, children could become less strained by the prison environment. However, if children are denied future visits, then their strain may continue. Along the same lines, mothers may have negative reactions to seeing their child leave the prison without them. However, repeated visits may help the mother cope with the pain of knowing that she is not currently able to provide and care for her child.

The small numbers of facilities that are available to females provide a special problem for incarcerated females. As a direct result of the small number of facilities, many females are imprisoned further away from their loved ones than their male counterparts are. There simply are not as many female prisons as there are male prisons. Males, on the average, will be incarcerated within a few hundred miles from their loved ones, while females will, on the average, be incarcerated beyond those same few hundred miles. This inadvertently places a greater strain on significant others of female inmates to drive further for a visit, take more time out of their day to visit their loved one, and even exhaust more resources such as money for gas, food, and hotel rooms that may be needed for excessively long journeys.

As a direct result of the limited number of prisons and female prisoners, there are also an insufficient number of resources available to them. Women's prisons are restricted in a variety of resources, including but not limited to personalized assessments, treatment for expecting mothers and violent offenders, vocational training (Wellisch, Anglin, & Prendergast, 1994), housing arrangements, individualized counseling, individualized or group treatments, and culturally diverse treatments (Law Library, n.d.). These restricted resources inevitably will also restrict all rehabilitative efforts in women's prisons. Moreover, when offered, many programs are restricted in their scope. For example, many vocational programs will offer traditional female stereotypical programs that will not translate to viable job opportunities once released, such as sewing, cosmetology, and even typing programs.

Like their male counterparts, drug offenders make up a large percentage of female inmates. However, unlike in men's prisons, there are relatively few drug programs that are available for women. The lack of rehabilitative drug programs not only affects rehabilitative efforts while in prison but undoubtedly will result in high reincarceration rates of inmates once released back into society.

CONCLUSION

Gender, femininity or masculinity alone does not automatically make up ones core beliefs. It does not assume that one gender is more ethically than the other. It does not even determine ones responsibilities. What gender does is allows individuals to occupy an identity that helps them to function in society authenticity. Likewise, sex, being male or female does not make one ethical or unethical. Factors like attitude, beliefs and thought create challenges to ethics. Therefore, occupationally standards, codes and guidelines are not based on sex or gender. They are character based, and determined based on operational factor. Which is why, the various waves of feminism have made numerous advancement in changing the conditions in which women have to face in society, the workplace and in the family. This has had a profound impact on the field on policing, courts, correctional supervision, and women inmates.

COPYRIGHTED MATERIAL — DO NOT DUPLICATE, DISTRIBUTE, OR POST

Discussion Questions

1 Should women be allowed to keep their newborn infants with them in prison for the first 2 years of the baby's life? Why or why not?

2 What other obstacles would women face if they pursued a career in law enforcement, law, or corrections?

REFERENCES

Adler, F., & Adler, H. M. (1975). *Sisters in crime: The rise of the new female criminal*. New York: McGraw-Hill.

Alpert, G., Dunham, R., & Stroshine, M. (2015). *Policing: Continuity and change*. Long Grove, IL: Waveland Press.

Braswell, M., McCarthy, B. R., & McCarthy, B. J. (2008). *Justice, crime, and ethics* (6th ed.). Cincinnati: Anderson.

Bureau of Justice Statistics. (1999). *Women offenders*. Washington, DC: US Government Printing Office.

Cheeseman, K., San Miguel, C., Frantzen, D., & Nored, L. (2011). *Everyday ethics for the criminal justice professional*. Durham, NC: Carolina Academic Press.

Epstein, C. (1988). *Deceptive distinctions: Sex, gender, and the social order*. New Haven, CT: Yale University Press.

Hagan, J. (1990). The structuration of gender and deviance: A power-control theory of vulnerability to crime and adolescent role exits. *Canadian Review of Sociology & Anthropology, 27*(2), 137–156.

Law Library. (n.d.). Prisons: Prisons for women—problems and unmet needs in the contemporary women's prison. Retrieved from http://law.jrank.org/pages/1805/Prisons-Prisons-Women-Problems-unmet-needs-in-contemporary-women-s-prison.html

Lilly, J., Ball, R., & Cullen, F. (2015). *Criminological theory: Context and consequences* (6th ed.). Thousand Oaks, CA: Sage.

Lonsway, K., Moore, M., Harrington, P., Smeal, E., & Spillar, K. (2003). *Hiring & retaining more women: The advantages to law enforcement agencies*. National Center for Women & Policing. Retrieved from http://womenandpolicing.com/pdf/nesadvantagesreport.pdf

Mallicoat, S. (2012). *Women and crime: A text/reader*. Thousand Oaks, CA: Sage.

Martin, S. E., & Jurik, N. C. (1996). *Doing justice doing gender: Women in law and criminal justice occupation*. London: Sage.

Menkel-Meadow, C. (2005). Portia redux: Another look at gender, feminism, and legal ethics. In S. D. Carle (Ed.), *Lawyers' ethics and the pursuit of social justice: A critical reader* (pp. 274–281). New York: New York University Press.

Potts, L. (1983). Equal employment opportunity and female employment in police agencies. *Journal of Criminal Justice, 11*, 505–523.

Sultan, C. G., & Townsey, R. D. (1981). *A progress report on women in policing*. Washington, DC.

Sykes, G. M. (1958). *The society of captives: A study of a maximum security prison*. Princeton, NJ: Princeton University Press.

Uniform Crime Reports. (2002). *Federal Bureau of Investigation, Crime in the United States, 2001*. Washington, DC: US Government Printing Office.

Wellisch, J., Anglin, M. D., & Prendergast, M. (1994). Treatment strategies for drug-abusing women offenders. In J. Inciardi (Ed.), *Drug treatment and the criminal justice system* (pp. 5–25). Thousand Oaks, CA: Sage.

COPYRIGHTED MATERIAL — DO NOT DUPLICATE, DISTRIBUTE, OR POST

COPYRIGHTED MATERIAL — DO NOT DUPLICATE, DISTRIBUTE, OR POST

8 | DRUG OFFENDERS

JENNIFER MEYER-BIDDLE, PhD

Reading Objectives

- Define the term *drug offender* and identify the impact that drug offenders have on the correctional system
- Identify the issues associated with housing a drug abuser
- Specify the criminal justice initiatives implemented in response to drug offenders entering the correctional system
- Identify the sentencing philosophies implemented for drug offenders
- Identify the types of substance-abuse programs provided for drug offenders in prison and in the community

---

OVERVIEW

Drug offenders have a significant impact on the correctional population. According to the Bureau of Justice Statistics, 16% of the state prison population were drug offenders in 2012 (Carson, 2014). For the federal prison population, drug offenders made up 51% of the federal prison population in 2013 (Carson, 2014). Approximately 25% of female prisoners and 15% of male prisoners were incarcerated for a drug offense (Carson, 2014).

Drug offenders also have a significant impact on community corrections. In 2013, 25% of the adults on probation were on probation for a drug offense, and 32% were on parole for a drug offense (Herberman & Bonczar, 2015).

In addition to being in the correctional system for a **drug-related crime**, there are a significant number of **drug abusers** in the criminal justice system. Based on the criteria stated in the fourth edition of the *Diagnostic and Statistical Manual of Mental Disorders*, 53% of state and 45% of federal prisoners met the criteria for drug dependence or abuse (Mumola & Karberg, 2006). Similarly, the Substance Abuse and Mental Health Services Administration (2014) reports that approximately 27% of the 1.7 million adults on supervised release from prison were current illicit drug users. For those on probation, roughly 31% were illicit drug users (Substance Abuse and Mental Health Services Administration, 2014).

Drug use also has a substantial impact on recidivism rate. In a study conducted by the Bureau of Justice Statistics that estimated the recidivism of over 400,000 individuals who were released from state prison in 2005, 76.9% of those committed for a drug offense were rearrested within 5 years of release (Durose, Cooper, & Snyder, 2014). Drug offenders continue to have one of the highest rates of recidivism.

COPYRIGHTED MATERIAL — DO NOT DUPLICATE, DISTRIBUTE, OR POST

COPYRIGHTED MATERIAL — DO NOT DUPLICATE, DISTRIBUTE, OR POST

Both drug abusers and offenders make up a substantial portion of the corrections, and they continue to demonstrate behavior that is often repeated. The American Society of Addiction Medicine (2011) indicates that the cycle of drug abuse involves persistent risk and an elevated likelihood of **relapse**.

As a result, drug use and drug-related crimes have had a significant impact on the criminal justice system. During the 1980s the United States experienced a drug epidemic due to the introduction of crack cocaine. In response to the drug epidemic, initial criminal justice initiatives focused on enhanced enforcement and incarceration (Peters & Murrin, 2000). The primary punishment philosophies instituted were **deterrence** and **incapacitation**. Due to the criminal justice response of enforcement and incarceration, an overwhelming number of drug offenders entered the courts, local jails, and prisons. In the court system, the influx of crack cocaine users into the criminal justice system presented a major crisis. The number of suspects prosecuted for drug offenses increased from 7,697 in 1981 to 25,663 in 1991 (Bureau of Justice Statistics, 1994). As a result, the percentage of offenders convicted for drug offenses rose from 73% in 1981 to 87% in 1991 (Bureau of Justice Statistics, 1994). For corrections, the percentage of state prisoners incarcerated for a drug offense was 6% in 1980 and rose to 23% by 1996 (U.S. Department of Justice, 1999). There was a similar increase for federal prisoners, 25% in 1980 and 60% in 1996 (U.S. Department of Justice, 1999). Adhering to the correctional philosophy of incapacitation, in many states parole boards were abolished and mandatory minimum sentences were instituted (Gebelein, 2001). In addition to being arrested and incarcerated for drug-related offenses, offenders were reporting high rates of illicit drug use. According to the Bureau of Justice Statistics (1999), 51% of the nation's prisoners reported the use of drugs while committing their offense. In 1997 over 80% of state and over 70% of federal prisoners reported past drug use, and about 1 in 6 of both groups reported committing their offense in order to obtain money for drugs.

The court system found itself unable to handle the heavy caseloads and unable to process offenders in a timely fashion, and local jails and prisons were becoming increasingly overcrowded. In an effort to address growing caseloads, courts employed delay-reduction strategies, including specialized court dockets, in order to expedite drug case processing (Bureau of Justice Statistics, 2003). Despite these efforts, substance-abusing adults repeatedly cycled through the judicial system.

The drug abuser poses a number of problems for corrections, including management, cost, and treatment. The management issues associated with chemical dependency must be addressed in jail, prison, probation, and parole. When an individual on drugs is arrested and detained, there is the potential for violent, unpredictable behavior. This presents a major control problem for the safety of both the correctional staff and the other detainees. In addition, upon being detained, drug abusers may experience withdrawal symptoms. Although the withdrawal symptoms for each drug vary, symptoms may include anxiety, headaches, depression, palpitations, and nausea (American Society of Addiction Medicine, 2011). More serious symptoms include heart attacks, stroke, and hallucinations (American Society of Addiction Medicine, 2011). In many instances, correctional staff lack the training to be able to identify and effectively treat withdrawal symptoms associated with drug use.

In addition to the management of drug abusers, drug offenders present substantial costs to the correctional system each year. According to the Vera Institute for Justice (Henrichson & Delaney, 2012), the annual cost of incarceration per inmate is $31,286. If one includes the police and court costs associated with the prosecution of drug offenders, the war on drugs costs taxpayers approximately $40 billion a year (Becker & Murphy, 2013). As a result, state and federal correctional institutions continue to develop innovative strategies to reduce recidivism for drug offenders. According to the Justice Policy Institute (2009), "treatment delivered in the community is one of the most cost-effective ways to prevent such crimes and costs approximately $20,000 less than incarceration per person per year" (p. 1).

Although many consider the treatment of drug offenders an essential component to reducing

COPYRIGHTED MATERIAL — DO NOT DUPLICATE, DISTRIBUTE, OR POST

drug-related offenses, there are a number of issues concerning the treatment of drug abusers in prison and in the community. One of the main goals of treating drug offenders is to provide evidence-based interventions, such as cognitive–behavioral therapy to instill positive coping skills and reinforce positive behavior changes. In addition, prison drug-treatment programs may include drug-abuse education classes or therapeutic communities, which are long-term, peer-led programs that use confrontational methods (National Institute on Drug Abuse, 2012). Unfortunately, only 15% of drug offenders receive treatment while incarcerated (National Institute on Drug Abuse, 2012). Although many criminal justice policies have imposed tougher sanctions on drug offenders and provided little treatment, the issue of treatment is important because effectively treating drug offenders provides an opportunity to decrease substance abuse and reduce associated criminal behavior. Since drug treatment in prison is not nearly enough to treat the population, treatment in the community—which includes short- and long-term residential programming, drug education classes, and self-help organizations such as Narcotics Anonymous—are essential. There are numerous studies that have found community-based treatments to be an effective mechanism to reduce drug use (Glasner-Edwards & Rawson, 2010; U.S. Department of Health and Human Services, 2000; Wallace, 2012).

CONTROVERSIAL ISSUES

There has been a variety of drug policies and sentencing strategies that have contributed to the current processing and treatment of drug offenders. Previous policies and strategies have contributed to the current state of corrections, while current and future practices seek to reduce the negative impact that has occurred.

DRUG POLICY

During the 1980s the United States' crime rates increased dramatically, many of which were drug offenses. In order to combat the influx of crime, a number of federal acts were passed by Congress, including the Comprehensive Crime Control Act of 1984, the Anti-Drug Abuse Act of 1986, and the Anti-Drug Abuse Act of 1988, which increased federal penalties for drug possession and applied mandatory sentences for drug-related crimes. Specifically, the Anti-Drug Abuse Acts of 1986 and 1988 established three-strikes provisions that instituted life sentences for repeat drug offenders. A report released by the Federal Judicial Center that provided a snapshot of mandatory minimums in 1992 revealed that over 38,000 offenders were sentenced under the guidelines, and over 40% of these were for drug-related crimes (Vincent & Hofer, 1994). As a result of years of similar sentences being applied, the incarceration rate continued to rise. After over 3 decades of punitive policies toward drug offenders, states have recently begun to reevaluate mandatory sentences. Nearly half of the states have amended statutes that applied a mandatory sentence of life imprisonment without parole for distribution of a drug such as cocaine or heroin (Stevenson, 2011). Since approximately 40% of those on probation and parole receive technical violations for recent drug use, a number of states have limited the length of incarceration that can be applied for these violations and are opting for drug therapy and counseling programs as an alternative (Stevenson, 2011). A number of states have also explored the decriminalization of certain drug offenses. **Decriminalization** is the abolition of criminal penalties in relation to certain acts, in this case, drug offenses (Drug Policy Alliance, 2016). According to the Drug Policy Alliance (2016), criminal penalties have been reduced or eradicated for personal marijuana possession in twenty states and Washington, DC and three states have reclassified possession from a felony to a misdemeanor for possession of small amounts of drugs like cocaine and heroin.

DISCRIMINATORY ENFORCEMENT

There is research evidence that enforcement of drug policies is racially discriminatory (Stevenson, 2011; Alexander, 2010). Enforcing drug laws by targeting specific communities that have high rates of minority citizens has contributed to the racial discrimination that minorities face. According to Stevenson (2011), African Americans make up 14% of drug users in the United States, but

COPYRIGHTED MATERIAL — DO NOT DUPLICATE, DISTRIBUTE, OR POST

COPYRIGHTED MATERIAL — DO NOT DUPLICATE, DISTRIBUTE, OR POST

they are 37% of those arrested for drug offenses and 56% of those that are incarcerated for drug offenses. Sentences for illegal possession or use of crack cocaine—which is more prevalent in communities of color—were 100 times greater than possession or use of equivalent amounts of powder cocaine, contributing to racially disparate sentencing, including longer prison sentences for African Americans (Stevenson, 2011). Although the law was amended in 2010, the law was not retroactive, so offenders already sentenced under the law remained in prison (Stevenson, 2011).

SENTENCING STRATEGIES

During the 1950s **rehabilitation** was viewed as the primary sentencing goal for drug offenders. Many programs addressing the offenders' needs were created (Gebelein, 2001). Programs were designed to diagnose the deficiencies that led to the committing of crime and to provide offenders with job training and education. During the 1970s the effectiveness of rehabilitation came under scrutiny, and many programs were considered a failure (Gebelein, 2001). According to Gebelein (2001), this occurred because correctional systems tried to rehabilitate offenders without knowing why people commit specific crimes, and discretion was seen to defeat fairness in sentencing.

By the early 1990s rehabilitation had faded as the primary sentencing goal, and **incapacitation** became principal. In many states parole boards were abolished, and **mandatory minimum sentences** were instituted (Gebelein, 2001). Although mandatory penal laws have been used since the 1800s, during the 1970s and 1980s the U.S. Congress and many states passed legislation that required judges to assign mandatory sentences for specific types of drug offenses (Justice Policy Institute, 2010). As a result, the number of sentences for drug-related offenses increased dramatically. Judges were now required to assign prison sentences rather than having the discretion to customize an appropriate sentence (Justice Policy Institute, 2010).

SENTENCING REFORM

Policies such as mandatory minimums and three-strikes laws have contributed to the high rate of drug offenders who are now incarcerated. Due to the high cost of incarceration, prison overcrowding, and the high recidivism rate of drug offenders, states and the federal government have begun to depart from mandatory sentences and other harsh strategies for drug offenses and move toward alternative models, such as harm reduction strategies and rehabilitation. For many states the expense associated with incarceration reduces resources for other vital services, including education and health care (Justice Policy Institute, 2010; Stevenson, 2011).

HARM REDUCTION

Harm reduction strategies encourage treatment and education for drug-related crimes. Specifically, harm reduction strategies focus on illegal drug use as a health problem in need of treatment rather than penalizing an individual through incarceration (Stevenson, 2011). Those who support crime reduction strategies recognize the need for incarceration in certain situations, including drug-trafficking offenses, but contend that drug use offenses should be met with treatment rather than penalties. A number of states have begun to acknowledge the benefits of harm reduction strategies and have started to allocate resources that emphasize education and treatment (Stevenson, 2011).

REHABILITATION

According to Spohn (2002), the goal of rehabilitation is crime prevention. "Rehabilitation does not achieve this goal by making the offender fearful of additional punishment (deterrence), or by isolating him so that his opportunities for crime are limited (incapacitation), but does so by reforming him" (Spohn, 2002, p. 13). In terms of punishment, the nature and duration should depend on the individual person's need until the offender is cured (Spohn, 2002). Numerous studies have found that drug treatment is more cost-effective than incarceration (National Institute on Drug Abuse, 2012; Wallace, 2012; Stevenson, 2011).

Treatment programs include evidence-based interventions, such as cognitive–behavioral therapy and contingency-management approaches, medications, and needle-exchange programs. In addition, drug-treatment courts have become an effective strategy to meet the needs of drug offenders.

COPYRIGHTED MATERIAL — DO NOT DUPLICATE, DISTRIBUTE, OR POST

COPYRIGHTED MATERIAL — DO NOT DUPLICATE, DISTRIBUTE, OR POST

Evidence-based interventions such as **cognitive–behavioral therapy** help offenders learn positive social and coping skills (National Institute on Drug Abuse, 2012). Similarly, **contingency-management approaches** promote and reinforce positive behavioral change to increase treatment engagement and program retention through motivational enhancement (National Institute on Drug Abuse, 2012). Medications such as **methadone** are used for those suffering from opiate addictions; these regulate brain activity to promote abstinence (National Institute on Drug Abuse, 2012). In addition, needle-exchange programs allow injecting drug users to obtain clean needles and propose treatment opportunities. Needle-exchange programs help reduce the rate of HIV infection and other infectious disease (Stevenson, 2011).

Drug-treatment courts have been instrumental in altering the traditional processing and subsequent treatment of drug offenders. The underlying principle for the establishment of **drug-treatment courts** has been that traditional methods such as incarceration have been inefficient (Belenko, 2001; Fischer, 2003; Stevenson, 2011). The goal of the drug-treatment courts is to rehabilitate rather than punish drug-addicted offenders, and thus to reduce drug use, recidivism, and social cost (Fischer, 2003). The court system works in conjunction with the drug offender to mandate drug-treatment and community-based programs. The primary aim is to provide treatment, not punishment, and the goals are to reduce drug use, promote sobriety, increase accountability, reduce recidivism, reduce the social cost of crime and drug use in a society, and promote positive behavior and social outcomes. Drug courts play an important role in redirecting drug offenders away from traditional methods of incarceration. According to Belenko (2001), drug courts are a method to deliver long-term court-supervised treatment to drug offenders and drug users. Similarly, Stevenson (2011) maintains that drug-treatment courts guard offenders from being incarcerated, which reduces prison overcrowding. In addition, treatment provided by drug courts reduces recidivism and promotes positive outcomes, such as increased employment, decreased medical expenses, and increased housing and family stability (Belenko, 2001; Gottfredson, Najaka, & Kearley, 2003; Spohn, Piper, Martin, & Frenzel, 2001).

CONCLUSION

The management and treatment of drug offenders has been an ongoing issue for decades. While earlier policies focused on more punitive methods of punishment, such as mandatory minimum sentences and three-strikes policies, current policies are exploring more rehabilitative models of treatment. Punitive policies that have contributed to overcrowding of prisons, the rise in prison costs, and high recidivism rates have forced government officials and correctional facilities to explore alternative methods of punishment. Similarly, because of the numerous problems that the current policies present to corrections, practitioners and researchers continuously look at new and innovative strategies to reduce the effect that drug offenders have on the current system. Current policies for drug offenders seek to reduce the punitive impact of previous policies by promoting the rehabilitation philosophy. There are many rehabilitative programs that have been beneficial in reducing the rate of recidivism. Moving forward, the principal issues associated with the continued rehabilitation philosophy are public sentiment and cost. Although we have made great strides to change the societal perspective that rehabilitation is easy on offenders and that they are not receiving the punishment that they deserve, it is still a struggle. In addition, because the United States currently spends an exorbitant amount on corrections each year, rehabilitation programs are often underfunded. In order to fully embrace rehabilitation as the current punishment philosophy, practitioners, researchers, government officials, and citizens need to work together to continue to implement comprehensive, effective rehabilitative strategies.

COPYRIGHTED MATERIAL — DO NOT DUPLICATE, DISTRIBUTE, OR POST

COPYRIGHTED MATERIAL — DO NOT DUPLICATE, DISTRIBUTE, OR POST

Discussion Questions

1 How do drug offenders impact the correctional system?

2 What are the issues associated with housing a drug abuser?

3 What are the sentencing philosophies that have been utilized with drug offenders?

4 What are the various treatment options available for drug offenders?

REFERENCES

Alexander, M. (2010). *The new Jim Crow: Mass incarceration in the age of colorblindness*. New York: New Press.

American Society of Addiction Medicine. (2011). *Definition of addiction*. Chevy Chase, MD: Author.

Anti-Drug Abuse Act of 1986, H.R. 5484 (99th) (1986).

Anti-Drug Abuse Act of 1988, H.R. 5210 (100th) (1988).

Becker, G., & Murphy, K. (2013, January 4). Have we lost the war on drugs? *Wall Street Journal*. Retrieved from https://www.wsj.com/articles/SB100014241278873243 74004578217682305605070

Belenko, S. (2001). *Research on drug courts: A critical review: 2001 update*. New York: National Center on Addiction and Substance Abuse.

Bureau of Justice Statistics. (1994). *Drug and crime facts, 1994*. Washington, DC: US Department of Justice.

Bureau of Justice Statistics. (1999). *Substance abuse and treatment, state and federal prisons, 1997*. Washington, DC: US Department of Justice.

Bureau of Justice Statistics. (2003). *Prevalence of imprisonment in the U.S. population, 1974–2001*. Washington, DC: US Department of Justice.

Carson, A. E. (2014). *Prisoners in 2013* (NCJ247282). Washington, DC: Bureau of Justice Statistics.

Comprehensive Crime Control Act, S.Rept 98-225 Part 1; S.Rept 98-241 Part 1 (1984).

Drug Policy Alliance. (2016). *Approaches to decriminalizing drug use & possession*. New York: Author. Retrieved from https://www.google.com/url?sa=t&rct=j&q=&esrc=s&source=web&cd=1&cad=rja&uact=8&ved=0ahUKEwjXkOyki8LbAhXSjVkKHfxCC40QFggnMAA&url=https%3A%2F%2Fwww.drugpolicy.org%2Fsites%2Fdefault%2Ffiles%2FDPA%2520Fact%2520Sheet_Approaches%2520to%2520Decriminalization_%2528Feb.%25202016%2529_0.pdf&usg=AOvVaw0yuq9hFQe1ANQmEWHh98lz

Durose, M. R., Cooper, A. D., & Snyder, H. N. (2014). *Recidivism of prisoners released in 30 states in 2005: Patterns from 2005 to 2010*. Washington, DC: US Department of Justice.

Fischer, B. (2003). Doing good with a vengeance. *International Journal of Policy and Practice, 3*(3), 227–248.

Gebelein, R. (2001). *Sentencing & corrections: The rebirth of rehabilitation: Promise and perils of drug courts*. Washington, DC: US Department of Justice.

Glasner-Edwards, S., & Rawson, R. (2010). Evidence-based practices in addiction treatment: Review and recommendations. *Health Policy, 97*(2–3), 93–104.

Gottfredson, D. C., Najaka, S. S., & Kearley, B. (2003). Effectiveness of drug treatment courts: Evidence from a randomized trial. *Journal of Drug Issues, 2*(2), 171–196.

Henrichson, C., & Delaney, R. (2012). *The price of prisons: What incarceration costs taxpayers* (Report, Vera Institute of Justice). Retrieved from https://www.vera.org/publications/price-of-prisons-what-incarceration-costs-taxpayers

Herberman, E. J., & Bonczar, T. P. (2015). *Probation and parole in the United States, 2013* (NCJ248029). Washington, DC: Bureau of Justice Statistics.

Justice Policy Institute. (2008). *Substance abuse treatment and public safety*. Washington, DC: Author.

Justice Policy Institute. (2009). *Pruning prisons: How cutting corrections can save money and protect public safety*. Washington, DC: Author.

Justice Policy Institute. (2010). *How to safely reduce prison populations and support people returning to their communities*. Washington, DC: Author.

Mumola, C., & Karberg, J. (2006). *Drug use and dependence, state and federal prisoners, 2004*. Washington, DC: Bureau of Justice Statistics.

COPYRIGHTED MATERIAL — DO NOT DUPLICATE, DISTRIBUTE, OR POST

COPYRIGHTED MATERIAL — DO NOT DUPLICATE, DISTRIBUTE, OR POST

National Institute on Drug Abuse. (2012). *Principles of drug abuse treatment for criminal justice populations: A research-based guide* (Publication No. 11-5316). Bethesda, MD: Author.

Peters, R. H., & Murrin, M. R. (2000). Effectiveness of treatment-based drug courts in reducing criminal recidivism. *Criminal Justice and Behavior, 27*(1), 72–96.

Spohn, C. (2002). *How do judges decide?* Thousand Oaks: CA: Sage.

Spohn, C., Piper, R. K., Martin, T., & Frenzel, E. D. (2001). Drug courts and recidivism: The results of an evaluation using two comparison groups and multiple indicators of recidivism. *Journal of Drug Issues, 31*(1), 149–176.

Stevenson, B. (2011). *Drug policy, criminal justice and mass imprisonment* (Working Paper). Geneva: Global Commission on Drug Policies.

Substance Abuse and Mental Health Services Administration. (2014). *Results from the 2013 National Survey on Drug Use and Health: Summary of National Findings* (NSDUH Series H-48, HHS Publication No. SMA 14-4863). Rockville, MD: Author.

US Department of Health and Human Services. (2000). *Changing the conversation, improving substance abuse treatment: The National Treatment Plan Initiative*. Washington, DC: Center for Substance Abuse Treatment.

US Department of Justice. (1999). *Prisoners in 1997*. Washington, DC: Bureau of Justice Statistics.

Vincent, B. S., & Hofer, P. J. (1994). *The consequences of mandatory minimum prison terms: A summary of recent findings*. Washington, DC: Federal Judicial Center.

Wallace, B. C. (2012). Controversies in knowledge translation for community-based drug treatment: The need to end policies of the war on drugs and mass incarceration of drug offenders to achieve health. *Equity Journal of Urban Health, 89*(6), 894–904.

COPYRIGHTED MATERIAL — DO NOT DUPLICATE. DISTRIBUTE. OR POST

COPYRIGHTED MATERIAL — DO NOT DUPLICATE, DISTRIBUTE, OR POST

COPYRIGHTED MATERIAL — DO NOT DUPLICATE. DISTRIBUTE. OR POST

COPYRIGHTED MATERIAL — DO NOT DUPLICATE, DISTRIBUTE, OR POST

9 | MENTAL HEALTH ISSUES

ALICIA SINGH, PhD

Reading Objectives

- Recognize and apply ethical standards to resolve conflicts with the mentally ill population
- Understand and identify ethically questionable human rights issues that arise when managing the mentally ill

---

OVERVIEW

Offenders with mental illnesses (OMIs) present several ethical challenges to the criminal justice system. Chapter 9 builds on previous chapters by illustrating the ethical challenges of processing and managing individuals with mental illnesses. Unlike "normal" offenders (those with no mental impairments), OMIs suffer from extensive "psychological impairments in their thought processes (e.g., delusions), sensory input (e.g., hallucinations), mood balance (e.g., mania or severe depression), memory (e.g., dementia), or the ability to reason, which interferes with their ability to meet the ordinary demands of living" (Treatment Advocacy Center, 2014, p. 108). Today millions of Americans suffer from some form of mental disorder and with treatment and medication can maintain a normal lifestyle. However, untreated mental disorders can have devastating effects on an individual's psychological and behavioral health, which in many cases can lead to homelessness, violent behavior, and incarceration. "The mentally ill offender represents a substantial challenge to the judicial, correctional and mental health systems"

(Freeman & Roesch, 1989, p. 114). Since, laws can sometimes contradict ethical principles, it is imperative that criminal justice professionals recognize and apply ethical standards to resolve conflicts with the mentally ill population. From a judicial perspective, the moral decision on whether to convict the mentally ill or divert to alternate sanctions, from a correctional standing, ethical concerns about housing and solitary confinement are major concerns, and from a mental-health system perspective, quality of care, and access to treatment issues arise.

According to the mens rea principle of criminal law, to hold an individual criminally responsible and accountable, a "guilty mind" must be established before the court. However, if any mental impairments are detected, the offender cannot be liable or punished by his act or omission (Lerner & Wilmoth Lerner, 2005). Despite, the mens rea declaration, OMIs are overrepresented in the prison population, which is simply the aggregate result of incompetent decision makers and unethical decisions (Pawel, 2001). The first section of this chapter examines the prevalence of mental illnesses in the criminal justice system, specifically the deinstitutionalization movement, which contributed

COPYRIGHTED MATERIAL — DO NOT DUPLICATE. DISTRIBUTE. OR POST

COPYRIGHTED MATERIAL — DO NOT DUPLICATE, DISTRIBUTE, OR POST

to an influx of mentally ill individuals released into the community from mental hospitals with inadequate postdischarge treatment, ultimately resulting in the criminalization movement. The second section examines general service delivery issues (i.e., quality of care and access to treatment) and solitary confinement. The chapter concludes with recommendations for balancing public safety without impinging on the constitutional rights of the mentally ill.

PATHWAY INTO THE CRIMINAL JUSTICE SYSTEM

From the 1870s through the early 1960s, the emphasis was on rehabilitation and treatment of the criminally insane, so instead of sending the mentally ill to prison, these individuals were committed to mental hospitals (Treatment Advocacy Center, 2007). However, in 1963 President John F. Kennedy signed the Community Mental Health Centers Act into law, which encouraged the closure of state hospitals—known as deinstitutionalization. The goal was to shift individuals from long-term psychiatric facilities to community-based centers to promote an independent living environment (Krieg, 2001), in hopes that the new setting would offer individuals the freedom and opportunity to sustain themselves in the community so they could lead productive lives. Under this model services were shifted from a "centralized system, managed through a state mental health authority, to a more diffuse system that consists of a range of payers, funding streams, and service providers" (Lurigio & Harris, n.d., p. 7). However, the centralization of psychiatric facilities resulted in a large portion of OMIs being released into the community with inadequate outpatient treatment, insufficient community resources, and insufficient 24-hour psychiatric care facilities (Lamb & Weinberger, 1998). Deinstitutionalization was an unequivocal promise to support OMIs with housing and mental health services, but poor planning left a large portion of severely mentally ill individuals with inadequate follow-up mental health treatment and housing. Unable to participate in the community, these individuals wound up homeless and destitute on the streets (Belcher, 1989; Gostin, 2008), creating the NIMBY (not in my backyard) syndrome (Krieg, 2001). Public perception is that individuals with mental illnesses are dangerous; these negative connotations and the NIMBY phenomenon create a barrier to opportunities for individuals with mental illness (Borinstein, 1992). Police, courts, and legislatures have implemented an increasingly punitive approach to individuals who do not fit within societal norms (Sentencing Project, 2002). And, since OMIs are prone to aberrant behavior that contravenes societal rules, they are often arrested for "quality of life" crimes (Sentencing Project, 2002) as a means of social control. Once in custody, the mentally ill represent a high-risk, high-need population that falls near the bottom of the social hierarchy (Freeman & Roesch, 1989).

CONTROVERSIAL ISSUES

What happens next can only be classified as the *criminalization of the mentally ill*, which shifts the mentally ill from mental health systems to the criminal justice system (Teplin, 1983). The criminalization begins at the point of arrest with the arresting officer, because without proper training, disruptive behavior could easily be mistaken for criminal behavior rather than mental illness, and the OMIs are referred to jail instead of a mental hospital (Quanbeck, Frye, & Altshuler, 2003). For example, individuals found unfit to stand trial are usually placed in a designated mental health facility until they become mentally fit to stand trial (Freeman & Roesch, 1989). However, the current trend contradicts the mens rea principle, because even though OMIs are mentally "unfit" for prison, they are continually diverted into the criminal justice system for punishment instead of a mental health institution for treatment.

Teplin (1984) conducted a 14-month observational study on the arresting practices of Chicago police officers to determine if there were any variations in arrest patterns among OMIs versus individuals with no mental illnesses. She found 46.7% of OMIs were arrested, compared to 27.9% of non-OMIs. Table 9.1 illustrates the mental health population in state, federal, and local jails in the United States. In 2005 individuals with any mental problems were 28.4% more likely to be incarcerated in jails than individuals with no mental conditions.

COPYRIGHTED MATERIAL — DO NOT DUPLICATE, DISTRIBUTE, OR POST

COPYRIGHTED MATERIAL — DO NOT DUPLICATE, DISTRIBUTE, OR POST

TABLE 9.1 U.S. 2005 Mental Health Prison Population from Local, State, and Federal Prisons

Mental health problem	State prison inmates		Federal prison inmates		Local jail inmates	
	Number	Percentage	Number	Percentage	Number	Percentage
Any mental health problem	705,600	56.2%	70,200	44.8%	479,900	64.2%
History and symptoms	219,700	17.5%	13,900	8.9%	127,800	17.1%
History only	85,400	6.8%	7,500	4.8%	26,200	3.5%
Symptoms only	396,700	31.6%	48,100	30.7%	322,900	43.2%
No mental health problem	549,900	43.8%	86,500	55.2%	267,600	35.8%

Source: James and Glaze (2006).

State prisons had 255,700 more OMIs than local jails over the same period (see Table 9.1).

"Correctional institutions have become the *de facto* state hospitals, and there are more seriously and persistently mentally ill individuals in prison that in all state hospitals in the United States (Daniel, 2007). The Treatment Advocacy Center (2014) estimates there were over 356,000 individuals with serious mental illnesses incarcerated in the prison and/or jail system in 2012. This is equivalent to the population of cities such as Anchorage, Alaska; Montgomery, Alabama; Peoria, Illinois; or Trenton, New Jersey. The report implies that prisons and jails have become the "new" asylums due to the number of individuals with serious mental illness being incarcerated. To put this into perspective, the rate individuals with mental illnesses in jails and prisons is 2 to 4 times higher than rate of individuals with mental illnesses found among the public (National Commission on Correctional Health Care, 2002). This is a disturbing trend, since the criminal justice system does not have adequate resources to treat or manage OMIs, which over the years has been a controversial human rights issue for policy administrators. A 1992 study of American jails reported that 29% of the jails admitted to detaining mentally ill individuals with *no charges* against them (Torrey, National Alliance for the Mentally Ill, & Public Citizen Health Research Group, 1992). From an ethical standpoint, there is absolutely no justification for detaining an individual without cause, because having a mental impairment is not a crime. To this end, the criminal justice system is not equipped or able to provide mental health services to the OMIs in its custody (Quanbeck et al., 2003, p. 1249), because it lacks the resources to provide proper treatment.

Under no circumstances should the criminal justice system be viewed as a substitute for the mental health system; to incarcerate an individual under these circumstances is ethically immoral and unconstitutional. The next section highlights the ethical challenge of providing effective treatment and rehabilitation services for the mentally ill.

ACCESS TO TREATMENT

While incarcerated, the mentally ill often need extra medical attention, treatment, medication, security, suicide precautions, special programming, rehabilitative services, case management, or transition services (Hills, Siegfried, & Ickowitz, 2004). But most correctional facilities do not have qualified mental health professionals to treat and respond to the needs of OMIs. A study by the National Institute of Justice (2007) found mental health programs in prisons were "grossly understaffed" and "in urgent need" of program development and of intervention by mental health organizations. Left untreated, the mental condition deteriorates, resulting in severe psychotic episodes of behavioral issues and violence. Access to care is a basic human right, and the availability—or lack of availability—to mental health services in the criminal justice system is ethically questionable (Quanbeck et al., 2003); from a human rights perspective, this is considered cruel and inhuman.

A comprehensive review of research on criminal justice programs revealed that only about 51%

COPYRIGHTED MATERIAL — DO NOT DUPLICATE, DISTRIBUTE, OR POST

COPYRIGHTED MATERIAL — DO NOT DUPLICATE, DISTRIBUTE, OR POST

of state prisons provide 24-hour mental care, and approximately 40% of all individuals with severe mental illnesses are not receiving treatment at any given time (Beck & Maruschak, 2001; Treatment Advocacy Center, 1999). "The ethical dilemma also arises when the practitioners' beliefs conflict with what the prison system dictates" (Kaslow, 1980, pp. 6–7). Ethical dilemmas arise when individuals have different values and beliefs and increase when resources are scarce. To protect human rights and safeguard against ineffective mental health service delivery systems, effective policies and procedures must be in place that provide the basic core screens; to refer, evaluate, designate, and continuously improve the quality of service delivery at all levels (Hinton, 2014).

THE PREVALENCE OF SOLITARY CONFINEMENT

"Disciplinary segregation, administrative, *secure housing units* (SHU), special management units (SMU), segregation, supermax, control units or 'the hole'" (Treatment Advocacy Center, 2014, p. 14), are terms used to describe isolation units within in a correctional facility. Isolation can occur for any reason as determined by the correctional or administrative staff (Adams & Ferrandino, 2008). Placement in isolation is done to protect staff and other inmates from harmful behaviors, such as assault, while also protecting the OMI from self-harm and from being victimized by other inmates. The idea is that removing the mentally ill inmate to a special setting deescalates situations while maintaining order in the general prison population (Adams & Ferrandino, 2008). Because of their inability to conform to institutional rules, OMIs receive more disciplinary referrals to isolation (Kurki & Morris, 2001). In 2003 approximately one quarter of New York prisoners detained in solitary confinement were mentally ill, while prisoners with moderate to severe mental illnesses accounted for most individuals in isolation in Colorado prisons in 2013 (Treatment Advocacy Center, 2014). Solitary confinement has essentially become a long-term solution for the mentally ill, which can ultimately worsen psychotic symptoms (Treatment Advocacy Center, 2014). The psychological effects of confinement include visual and auditory hallucinations, paranoia, overt psychosis, anxiety, depression, and

lethargy—and these increase the risk of suicide (Cockrell, 2013).

The use of solitary confinement as a disciplinary measure for controlling aberrant behavior constitutes cruel, inhuman, or degrading treatment and is a violation of the International Covenant on Civil and Political Rights and the Convention Against Torture and Other Cruel, Inhuman or Degrading Treatment or Punishment (United Nations, 1984). The recommendation comes with a caveat urging states to ban solitary confinement because it contradicts rehabilitation goals of the prison system (Mendez, 2011). According to the Sentencing Project 2002 report, suicide rates among OMIs who previously attempted suicide are 100 times higher than the rate in the general population. Over 50% of jail suicides are committed within the first 24 hours in jail. More than 95% of those who commit suicide in correctional facilities have a treatable psychiatric illness (Sentencing Project, 2002).

In 2000, 17-year-old Armando Cruz attacked a California Highway Patrol Officer with a knife from behind. It should be known that Armando had a long history of mental illnesses, including schizophrenia and aggression. In 2002 Cruz was found guilty of attempted murder and sentenced to life in prison, despite contradicting the mens rea principle. Ultimately, after spending years in solitary confinement, Cruz committed suicide in 2011. The death of Cruz was a culmination of years in solitary confinement and self-harming behavior (Rodriguez, 2013). This case is one of thousands that exemplify the psychological effects solitary confinement has on individuals with severe mental illnesses. Despite these growing concerns, there are approximately 60 supermax prisons housing more than 20,000 prisoners, with a large portion of OMIs disproportionately overrepresented in solitary confinement (Cockrell, 2013). Solitary confinement is a conscious decision by prison officials to isolate individuals for extended periods unjustly and without cause (Metzner & Fellner, 2010). Prisons are governed by strict rules, which the mentally ill cannot comprehend (Wachtler & Bagala, 2013), and those who violate these rules are reprimanded to total isolation as a disciplinary measure. Once in isolation, the mentally ill are often left untreated or undertreated, causing their

COPYRIGHTED MATERIAL — DO NOT DUPLICATE. DISTRIBUTE. OR POST

COPYRIGHTED MATERIAL — DO NOT DUPLICATE, DISTRIBUTE, OR POST

conditions to deteriorate (Wachtler & Bagala, 2013).

One of the major ethical dilemmas with solitary confinement is the absence of disciplinary hearings or due process preliminary hearings prior to confinement (Wachtler & Bagala, 2013). Critics argue that solitary confinement is a violation of Eighth Amendment rights and have filed numerous lawsuits over the years, claiming unwarranted punishment of persons with mental illness, abuse, humiliation, and neglect of medical treatment. "Prisoners are sent to prison as punishment and not for punishment" (Lemmergaard & Muhr, 2009, p. 42), and if we accept the fact that the mentally ill need to be confined as a safety precaution to avoid self-harm or harm to others, then the important question is how to respond humanely and constructively to the need, instead of caging OMIs in inhumane conditions (Pawel, 2001).

CONCLUSION

The treatment of the mentally ill is a direct result of a long-standing penal philosophy of maintaining order and discipline by severely punishing those who are disruptive or fail to conform to the rules (Gostin, 2008). Ethics is important for managing the mentally ill because it reduces the "unnecessary, unjust and harmful imprisonment of offenders with mental disabilities" (Fraser, Gatherer, & Hayton, 2009, p. 413). The research illustrates a strong correlation between treatment and control, so finding an appropriate balance between the two objectives is a critical management issue for policy administrators (Adams & Ferrandino, 2008). Although administrators are aware of the ethical challenges of managing OMIs, they often lack the moral prudence, compassion, and ethical decision-making skills (Hylton, 1995) necessary to make decisions in a responsible and ethical manner. An understanding of ethics is important when handling the mentally ill because without knowledge of ethics, criminal justice professionals may be naive about moral issues related to due process, discretionary decisions, and the use of force.

Prisons are not a dumping ground for the mentally ill (Fraser et al., 2009), and the barbaric practice of incarcerating the mentally ill is unethical and inhumane. Efficacy and effectiveness can only be achieved when the criminal justice system is operating in an ethical manner. To achieve this goal, administrators must develop new policies aimed at diverting the flow of the mentally ill from the prisons and jails and into treatment settings (Quanbeck et al., 2003). Recommendations for improving the current system include reforming laws and practices, increasing mental health services to the mentally ill, and implementing jail-diversion programs to reduce the number of individuals with mental illnesses from entering the prison system. We also challenge criminal justice professionals to be cognizant of ethical issues, employ critical-thinking skills, and apply ethical decision-making skills in the decision-making process. The criminal justice system should operate and support fair, equitable treatment for all individuals, especially the mentally ill, and refrain from malfeasance, including criminalizing the mentally ill and solitary confinement. It is unjustified to sentence mentally ill individuals to prison, so instead of promoting policies that support the "revolving door" phenomenon (Quanbeck et al., 2003), administrators should work to ensure OMIs are diverted away from prisons and into appropriate treatment facilities. "Until the extent of the problem is better delineated and creative solutions found, it seems likely that mentally ill offenders will be as much at risk from society as they will be a risk to society" (Freeman & Roesch, 1989, p. 114).

COPYRIGHTED MATERIAL — DO NOT DUPLICATE. DISTRIBUTE. OR POST

Discussion Questions

1 Why is ethics important in the management of the mentally ill population?

2 What are sources of possible ethical dilemmas associated with managing and treating mentally ill persons in the criminal justice system?

3 How can an ethical framework help criminal justice administrators make appropriate and moral decisions?

4 How can the competing criminal justice goals (retribution versus rehabilitation) be reconciled to meet the needs of mentally ill offenders?

REFERENCES

Adams, K., & Ferrandino, J. (2008). Managing mentally ill inmates in prisons. *Criminal Justice and Behavior, 35*(8), 913–927. doi:10.1177/0093854808318624

Beck, A. J., & Maruschak, L. M. (2001). *Mental health treatment in state prisons, 2000.* Bureau of Justice Statistics Special Report. Washington, DC: Government Printing Office.

Belcher, J. R. (1989). On becoming homeless: A study of chronically mentally ill persons. *Journal of Community Psychology, 17,* 173–185.

Borinstein, A. B. (1992). Public attitudes toward persons with mental illness. *Health Affairs, 11*(3), 186–196. doi:10.1377/hlthaff.11.3.186

Cockrell, J. F. (2013). Solitary confinement: The law today and the way forward. *Law and Psychology Review, 37,* 211.

Daniel, A. E. (2007). Care of the mentally ill in prisons: Challenges and solutions. *Journal of the American Academy of Psychiatry and the Law Online, 35*(4), 406–410.

Fraser, A., Gatherer, A., & Hayton, P. (2009). Mental health in prisons: Great difficulties but are there opportunities? *Public Health, 123*(6), 410–414. doi:10.1016/j.puhe.2009.04.005

Freeman, R. J., & Roesch, R. (1989). Mental disorder and the criminal justice system: A review. *International Journal of Law and Psychiatry, 12*(2), 105–115. doi:10.1016/0160-2527(89)90002-2

Gostin, L. O. (2008). "Old" and "new" institutions for persons with mental illness: Treatment, punishment or preventive confinement? *Public Health, 122*(9), 906–913.

Hills, H., Siegfried, C., & Ickowitz, A. (2004). *Effective prison mental health services: Guidelines to expand and improve treatment.* National Institute of Corrections. Retrieved from https://s3.amazonaws.com/static.nicic.gov/Library/018604.pdf

Hinton, M. (2014). Mentally ill offenders' impact on the prison system. *Disease-a-Month: DM, 60*(5), 213–214. doi:10.1016/j.disamonth.2014.04.003

Hylton, J. H. (1995). Care or control: Health or criminal justice options for the long-term seriously mentally ill in a Canadian province. *International Journal of Law and Psychiatry, 18*(1), 45–59.

James, D. J., & Glaze, L. E. (2006). *Mental health problems of prison and jail inmates.* Bureau of Justice Statistics. Retrieved from http://www.bjs.gov/content/pub/pdf/mhppji.pdf

Kaslow, F. W. (1980). Ethical problems in prison psychology. *Criminal Justice and Behavior, 7*(1), 3–9. doi:10.1177/009385488000700101

Krieg, R. G. (2001). An interdisciplinary look at the deinstitutionalization of the mentally ill. *Social Science Journal, 38*(3), 367–380. doi:10.1016/S0362-3319(01)00136-7

Kurki, L., & Morris, N. (2001). The purposes, practices, and problems of supermax prisons. *Crime and Justice: A Review of Research, 28,* 385–424.

Lamb, H. R., & Weinberger, L. E. (1998). Persons with severe mental illness in jails and prisons: A review. *Psychiatric Services, 49*(4), 483–492. doi:10.1176/ps.49.4.483

Lemmergaard, J., & Muhr, S. L. (2009). Treating threats: The ethical dilemmas of treating threatening patients. *Service Industries Journal, 29*(1), 35–45. doi:10.1080/02642060802116370

Lerner, K. L., & Wilmoth Lerner, B., (2005). *Mens rea: World of forensic science* (Vol. 2). Detroit: Gale.

COPYRIGHTED MATERIAL — DO NOT DUPLICATE, DISTRIBUTE, OR POST

Lurigio, A. R., & Harris, A. (n.d.). *The mentally ill in the criminal justice system: An overview of historical causes and suggested remedies.*

Mendez, J. E. (2011). Solitary confinement should be banned in most cases, UN expert says. United Nations News Centre. Retrieved from http://www.un.org/apps/news/story.asp?NewsID=40097

Metzner, J. L., & Fellner, J. (2010). Solitary confinement and mental illness in U.S. prisons: A challenge for medical ethics. *Journal of the American Academy of Psychiatry and the Law, 38,* 104–108.

National Commision on Correctional Health Care. (2002). *The health status of soon-to-be-released inmates: A report to Congress* (2 Vols.). Chicago: Author. Retrieved from http://ncchc.org/health-status-of-soon-to-be-released-inmates

National Institute of Justice. (2007). Mental health screens for corrections. Retrieved from https://www.ncjrs.gov/pdffiles1/nij/216152.pdf

Pawel, M. A. (2001). Imprisoning the mentally ill: Does it matter? *Criminal Justice Ethics, 20*(1), 2.

Quanbeck, C., Frye, M., & Altshuler, L. (2003). Mania and the law in California: Understanding the criminalization of the mentally ill. *American Journal of Psychiatry, 160*(7), 1245–1250.

Rodriguez, S. (2013). Suicide in solitary: The life and death of Armando Cruz (Part 1). Retrieved from http://solitarywatch.com/2013/01/17/suicide-in-solitary-the-life-and-death-of-armando-cruz-part-1

Sentencing Project. (2002). Mentally ill offenders in the criminal justice system: An analysis and prescription. Retrieved from http://www.sentencingproject.org/doc/publications/sl_mentallyilloffenders.pdf

Teplin, L. A. (1983). The criminalization of the mentally ill: Speculation in search of data. *Psychological Bulletin, 94*(1), 54–67. doi:10.1037/0033-2909.94.1.54

Teplin, L. (1984). Criminalizing mental disorder: The comparative arrest rate of the mentally ill. *American Psychologist, 39,* 794–803.

Torrey, E. F., National Alliance for the Mentally Ill, & Public Citizen Health Research Group. (1992). *Criminalizing the seriously mentally ill: The abuse of jails as mental hospitals, a joint report of the National Alliance For The Mentally Ill and Public Citizen's Health Research Group.* Washington, DC: Public Citizen's Health Research Group.

Treatment Advocacy Center. (1999). More mentally ill persons are in jails and prisons than hospitals: A survey of the states. Retrieved from http://www.treatmentadvocacycenter.org/storage/documents/final_jails_v_hospitals_study.pdf

Treatment Advocacy Center. (2007). Criminalization of individual with severe psychiatric disorders. Retrieved from http://www.treatmentadvocacycenter.org/GeneralResources/Fact3.htm

Treatment Advocacy Center. (2014). The treatment of persons with mental illness in prisons and jails: A state survery. Retrieved from http://www.treatmentadvocacycenter.org/storage/documents/treatment-behind-bars/treatment-behind-bars.pdf

United Nations. (1984). Convention against torture and other cruel, inhuman or degrading treatment or punishment. Retrieved from https://treaties.un.org/pages/viewdetails.aspx?src=treaty&mtdsg_no=IV-9&chapter=4&lang=en

Wachtler, S., & Bagala, K. (2013). From the asylum to solitary: Transinstitutionalization. *Albany Law Review, 77*(3), 915.

COPYRIGHTED MATERIAL — DO NOT DUPLICATE, DISTRIBUTE, OR POST

COPYRIGHTED MATERIAL — DO NOT DUPLICATE, DISTRIBUTE, OR POST

COPYRIGHTED MATERIAL — DO NOT DUPLICATE. DISTRIBUTE. OR POST

COPYRIGHTED MATERIAL — DO NOT DUPLICATE, DISTRIBUTE, OR POST

COPYRIGHTED MATERIAL — DO NOT DUPLICATE. DISTRIBUTE. OR POST

COPYRIGHTED MATERIAL — DO NOT DUPLICATE, DISTRIBUTE, OR POST

COPYRIGHTED MATERIAL — DO NOT DUPLICATE. DISTRIBUTE. OR POST